P9-DCZ-612

BORN ON FRIDAY 13TH

Anna Murray
April 2008

A Woman born on Friday the 13th struggles with a string of bad luck
and tragedy before finding a way to live with her fate.

Name   : Born on Friday 13th

ISBN   : 1440453403

EAN 13   : 9781440453403

Printer   : CreateSpace

Color   : B/W with Bleed

Country of
Publication   : United States

Author   : Anna Murray

Editor   : Ashley Mason

Cover Design : Wicked Sunny

Book Format   : Wicked Sunny
                (sunnykapoor@yakshacomics.com).

Edition 1

Contents

ACKNOWLEDGEMENT

I have so many people to thank for helping me get this book up and running: my cousin Nigel Walsh for filling me in with my father's family history, Richard Fawcus for my mother's side, my half-sister Mo Topper for little snippets. I also owe great debts to Bella Boyle (née Ryan) for her contributions and encouragement, and to the Hon. Vron Hodges for her pestering me to get on and get the book finished! A big thank you to Geoffrey Auckland for his poems on my "big" birthdays, and to all my customers at the Pub who told me I should write a book and have given me great encouragement. I couldn't have done it without the help of my wonderful editor, Ashley Mason from WordsRU, and Sunny who helped with my book cover and formatting the manuscript with photos. I would like to thank all those people who touched my life and made this story possible, and to my cousin Penny, who opened my eyes to the sharks on the Internet.

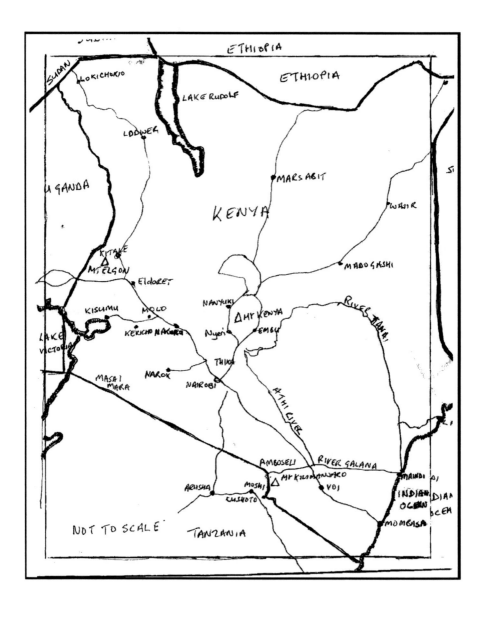

CHAPTER 1
KENYA

We will be landing in Nairobi in five minutes. The weather is hot and sunny.

The loudspeaker informed us of details of our landing. I was trembling with excitement: this was my first visit back to Kenya since I left Mombasa on a boat to Durban, South Africa, 27 years ago. I had persuaded my friend Diana to join my aunt Lois and me on a safari to Kenya, and was so looking forward to showing her my homeland.

As we stepped off the plane, that familiar African smell and warmth, not found anywhere else, hit me with such force, bringing back many cherished memories of my wonderful childhood. I had forgotten how I missed that hot acrid smell that was Africa: crossing the tarmac to the main airport building, I could hardly wait to see all the old places again.

Once we had checked through Customs, we loaded our bags into the waiting car and drove to our hotel. Horror of horrors, when we tried to check in to the hotel, we found we had been allocated one room with a double bed and one single bed. I could not imagine any one of us wanting to share a bed with another, and none of us volunteered it. Diana and I had agreed that we would share a room on the holiday, but we had specified two beds in each room we stayed in. With all of us being strong-willed characters, it wasn't long before Lois was allocated another room.

Early the next morning, we met our fellow companions on the safari. Hazel joined our bus, and two young couples in the other. The two safari buses set off in convoy for Amboseli, where we drove on unpaved roads towards Mt Kilimanjaro. We were all very excited to see animals, but only the occasional antelope and a herd of wildebeest grazing with zebra appeared.

"When are we going to see the lions and tigers?" Hazel enquired. Diana and I cracked up laughing, and Lois informed her in rather a superior voice,

"We don't have tigers in Africa!"

As we approached the hotel we could see smoke coming from a concrete pit which was obviously an incinerator; in the surrounding trees sat masses of marabou storks—ugly birds—hoping to find a morsel left out.

"Do they sit around there keeping warm?" asked Hazel.

"No, they are scavenging for bits that haven't been burnt," I replied.

"Oh yes, they are predators," Hazel announced. I looked at Diana and rolled my eyes: we could hardly contain ourselves. We realized we were in for a week of inane remarks.

As we entered the hotel Lois gave us a talking to, like we were two small children rather than two grown women in their thirties.

"Poor Hazel, this is her first trip abroad, now you mustn't pick on her!" She almost had us feeling sorry for her but we couldn't help smiling.

The hotel we stayed in was made up of individual lodges as rooms, and every morning we drove out early to see the animals at the watering holes. Our driver was heading in one direction and pointed out a huge pile of dung, and said there were elephants, probably very close.

"How do you know that?" asked Hazel.

"Well if you look carefully, you will see that it is fresh and almost steaming. That means they are not far away."

As he finished speaking, out of the undergrowth came two huge elephants that plodded across our path. The driver stopped so we could watch them, and he was standing where the roof opened and looked around.

"Look behind us, here is a male elephant!" as he got down into the driving seat again. "We need to be careful because we are between him and his two ladies."

As we were watching the male elephant, more elephants, including a baby, came out of the undergrowth. This was a frightening experience, as there were a whole bunch of elephants on either side of us, with "daddio" behind us. Hazel got really excited:

"Get us out of here!" she screeched. The driver asked her to calm down—we needed to keep very quiet. I think all our hearts were beating double-time. We had to trust our driver. As the elephants moved across our path, we watched, carefully keeping an eye on the bull. He seemed to get closer and then the driver saw the path was clear ahead, and he drove off slowly and the bull elephant seemed to follow us, picking up speed. The driver then accelerated and left the bull way behind. Once we were out of his reach we slowed down and watched the bull join the rest of the herd. It was almost too much excitement so early in the morning.

Driving back across the plains, our driver said there was a cheetah up ahead. We wondered how he knew.

"Do you see those zebra and gazelle all moving over there at quite a pace? That is usually because they can sense and smell a lion or cheetah. The lions tend to be a little higher, so they can see what is happening, but the cheetah is so fast he slinks along in the grass." We came to a cross track, and the driver slowed up to a standstill.

"Look over there. Do you see him? He is crouched in the grass." I had never seen such a mangy specimen. He was scarred and very thin, but the driver assured us that was normal for a wild cheetah. We watched him edge along on his belly and then, like a bolt, he was galloping across the plain towards the zebra and antelope. We noticed him go for the smallest young zebra and pulled him down very quickly. None of us wanted to watch anymore, so the driver continued back to the hotel.

On the third morning, we stepped out of our lodge to find ourselves knee-deep in water. We ran to the lounge where hot tea awaited us, to be told that the drive had been cancelled as all the roads were under water and impassable. Instead, we returned to our rooms and had our own spectacular view of animals coming down to the water's edge, which had been made from the dip in the land outside; it fed into our own private waterhole where all the animals came to us. We missed nothing: the elephants, giraffe, zebra and various bucks came to drink, and on the far side was a large thorn tree with a dozen vultures, hanging around like old men as they watched for any kills. When all was quiet, even a leopard was seen slinking up to the water. The thorn trees and remaining vultures were silhouetted against the fiery backdrop of the sky. Kenya's sunsets were something I remembered vividly from my childhood. The darkening night was crowded with the cries of a hyena calling its babes and the sound of hyraxes (well-furred rotund creatures with a stump of a tail, about the size of a corgi. They eat grass and leaves.) filled the air. In the far distance we could hear the throb of drums and the Africans chanting.

The following day after the rains had subsided and the roads became clear, we set off back to Nairobi, and were fortunate to have a spectacular view of the top of Mt Kilimanjaro with a large white ruff around its neck. Our driver said we were very lucky as it was rare to see the top of the mountain—it is usually covered in clouds.

When we reached our hotel we sorted our bags for the next safari to Masai Mara. The trip in itself was an experience I shall never forget. If we thought the roads to Amboseli were a bit rough, it was nothing to compare with this journey: we drove for miles and miles on the bed of the Rift Valley and there was nothing but flat land and strange thorn trees scattered across the surface. No hills, no greenery, no civilisation as far as the eye could see until we came to Narok, a shabby little village with a *duka* (shop) that sold carved wooden animals, and African crafts. The stench in the village was quite powerful, of open latrines, rotting meat and sweat. We stopped to buy cold drinks and freshen up, and to peruse the duka. Diana had her eye on a beautiful ebony hippo, but when we asked the price it was far too expensive and started to walk out—the Africans started chatting amongst themselves, and called us back.

"Make us an offer," one of them said. We started bartering, and they kept chatting amongst themselves. I was brought up in Ke-

nya, and picked up a good understanding of Swahili during my childhood; finally I blurted out,

"Mena sekia wena sema kitugani" (I understand what you are
saying). I told them I was born and brought up in Kenya, and they
were wringing our necks. They laughed and reduced the price, so
Diana got it for a very reasonable amount.

Before returning to the vans, Lois, Diana and I paid a visit to
the ladies' room. It was an extraordinary arrangement, made of cor-
rugated iron and a long concrete floor, with a step running the length
of the "room" on which the cubicles were placed. On opening the
door to a cubicle one was met with a white porcelain loo, buried in
the concrete up to its rim. Hanging above this was a rope to pull in
order to flush afterwards. I wonder why they went to such trouble to
bury the loo rather than just leaving it standing like most loos are. The
worst trap was the step just after the doors of the cubicles—when Lois
came out, she forgot it was there, and with her poor eye sight, fell in
a heap, cutting her leg on the filthy step. Horror of horrors, there was
no basin to wash your hands, so we couldn't even make a pretense of
cleaning it up; luckily, Diana had some alcohol in her medical kit, so
she washed the wound when we got back to the van.

We were travelling in convoy with another safari bus, and
after leaving Narok, the fun really started. We came to a "traffic jam"
in the middle of the bush! In front of us lay a road completely covered
in water for about fifty feet in front of us. All the traffic, the lorries,
safari buses, trucks and cars had veered off to the right, but they were
all stuck in the mud. Two vehicles had gone left and were also stuck;
we had no choice but to spend the next few hours waiting for them all
to get through before we could try.

"Ok, hold on, everyone," our driver said. "I am going to try and
go through the water!" So we held on and he drove like the clappers
through the water, which was about three feet deep. We hit a pothole
so hard I thought we were all going to be thrown out of the bus, but
the driver persisted and carried on. There was an incline upwards out
of the water, but with the acceleration he had given it we thought we

could make it—until a young Masai decided to cross our path with his
cattle. If we stopped we would be totally stuck, with no acceleration
to get us out. Diana was sitting in the front, and thinking very quickly,
she put her arm out, thumped on the side of the bus and bellowed,

"*Harembe, harembe!*"…Those cattle moved twice as fast as
they had intended and had cleared the way without the driver having
to slow down. We all breathed a sigh of relief.

The other safari bus followed us, and did not have the misfor-
tune to encounter cattle. On we went until we came to the next hazard.
Ahead of us was a clear road, no traffic, but up each side on their
own tracks were lorries, all stuck in the mud. Both buses stopped and
between us we had ten people and two vehicles to get up this hill. We
decided to take one vehicle at a time and put the lightest person in to
drive—my aunt—and the rest of us would push.

Nine of us pushed each vehicle up the hill. It was the most difficult slippery job I think I have ever encountered. Not only was it too
slippery for the vehicle, it was almost impossible for us to hold our
ground and push. This was the moment we should have had cameras
out. Each of us had fallen, and we were covered from head to foot
with mud. I have often wondered since why they don't have four-
wheel drives in Africa.

When we eventually arrived at the hotel we must have looked
a very sorry sight; but perhaps they were used to hotel guests arriving
like that!

The next bit of excitement came shortly after our arrival: I ran
water for a bath only to see it rush from the tap completely muddy
and brown. I screamed and Diana rushed in to find out if I had come
across a snake or something.

"No, look at the water." I said, "I feel I have come home.
Our water was always this colour; I had no idea that people actually
bathed in clear water until I went to South Africa when I was 12." We
rolled around laughing and Diana felt we had to have a picture of me
in the muddy bath.

Walking up to the dining room for dinner that evening we found hyraxes just walking up the path, not taking any notice of the humans. It was fascinating to be so close to nature. During the day when we swam in the pool we had to be careful of the monkeys, who would steal our drinks or any food we might be eating. They were actually quite a menace.

Masai Mara had every animal we could imagine. There were crocodiles, hippo, elephants, lions, cheetahs, leopards and every kind of buck, giraffe and buffalo. The drives were fascinating.

Our drivers took us to the crocodile and hippo pool. We found several other safari vans there and parked with them. This was about the most commercial place I had seen out in the wild—I almost expected to see a hot-dog or refreshment stand, but luckily we were spared that. We walked down through the undergrowth and came to a large pool in the river below us. In the middle of the pool, several hippos were huddled together with their heads under water and just showing a large mass of grey. There was a splash as one dived under and came up a few feet away.

On the far muddy bank we saw a movement, and what had looked like a log was a crocodile slithering into the water. Several other crocodiles followed suit. A herd of buffalo were approaching the water and had woken the sleepy crocs, as they came down to drink. We watched as a young calf came forward and in a flash, a crocodile grabbed the calf and dragged it into the water. The calf kicked and floundered and squealed and the mother charged the crocodile. She tossed it in the air, but at the same time the other crocodiles moved in and grabbed the young calf again. Several other buffalo came into the water to try and rescue the baby, but the crocodile had pulled it under water. The mother again tried to attack where she thought they were and her calf came up with the crocodile, trying to drag it back. Buffalo are ferocious animals, and she attacked again and we saw the crocodile tossed into the water, and the young calf staggered out onto

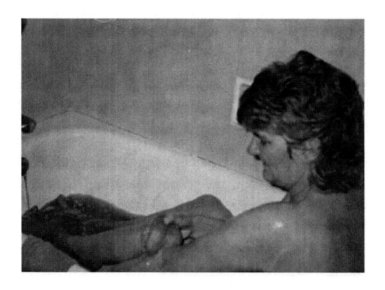

Taking a muddy bath at Masai Mara

Diana and Lois in the sweltering heat when the taxi broke
down

Hunt Meet at the Highlands Hotel, 1963

The Molo church, 1989 with Francis and Diana

The horses outside our bedroom at the Highlands Hotel,
1989

Anna and Diana having a drink outside the lounge, where
tea is served, 1989

the bank. That little calf put up such a fight. Our hearts were in our mouths watching this attack, and there was a great sigh of relief when once the calf was on the bank the older buffalo surrounded it and moved away.

While we were at the crocodile pool our drivers had been chatting with other drivers: on our return to the vans, they told us we would go and see some lions that the other drivers had told them about.

Masai Mara is vast, and very wild. We drove off through the savannah; after the rains the roads were under water and glistened in the sun. Ahead were two wheel tracks under water with grass running down the middle and either side. Our driver decided he would get a better grip by driving off the tracks on the grass.

After many miles he announced, "That is Tanzania over there," as he pointed to the many miles of savannah land ahead. "We are right on the border of Kenya and Tanzania."

We followed the tracks around and ahead we could see a small hill with some bushes, trees and rocks. We headed for the hillock rather cautiously and there lying in the sun were two lionesses. One lifted her head and put it down again; the other didn't move at all. As we glanced around we saw the male watching from a rock. We were very close to them and able to take some good photos. Returning back to the hotel, we saw giraffes eating from the high thorn trees and several ostriches were amongst them.

The following day we saw all the usual zebra, gazelle, dik diks, and giraffes and were rather disappointed that we didn't see any elephants, lions, or buffalo. Suddenly, our driver slowed down and said "Look over there. Do you see all that dust? It looks like a herd of buffalo are coming this way." Along the ridge we could see an enormous herd of buffalo and we were right in their path: our driver backed up, so that we would be down wind to the animals, and we waited. They came crashing through the undergrowth and passed 50 yards ahead of us. There were families of them with their young, probably 50 in all. They stopped to graze and looked up and then carried on their way. Our driver warned us to keep very quiet and let them pass, as aggravated buffalo can be very dangerous.

Luckily the rains had stopped and the roads had dried up on our way back to Nairobi. I found that our driver came from my village Molo, and had gone to the same school I went to, after Independence. I asked him if we shortened our visit to Malindi, could we hire him to drive us up to Molo, at the end of our visit. He agreed to this.

Kenya claimed its independence from Britain in 1963. Before that date, there was segregation with separate schools for Africans, whites and Indians, and separate hotels, shops and areas where they lived. Once Kenya achieved Independence and the new President, Jomo Kenyatta, took over from Britain, the name was changed from Kenya (pronounced Keenia) to Kenya as in Kenyatta, as it is now known.

On our return to Nairobi, we flew to Mombasa and then changed to a much smaller plane to fly to Malindi. Strangely enough a Concord was sitting on the runway at Mombasa, and when we were in the airport building we found the occupants. Someone had hired Concord for a trip around the world.

Malindi is where I spent my first four years of my life. My parents ran a *duka* (shop) called Murray's, selling everything from paraffin to shoelaces, as well as alcohol and food. We had an African *Ayah* (nanny) from birth, so my brother and I grew up speaking Swahili as our second language.

The shop was right across from the Eden Rock Hotel, where we learnt to swim before we could walk; I have memories of beautiful sandy beaches and swimming to the coral reef and snorkeling at the fish. We were safe from sharks, as they never cross the reef, but living on the coast brought a few horrors as well. My mother put my brother and I down to rest every afternoon, and one day when she went to pick my younger brother out of his cot, she found a python curled up in his cot. She quickly plucked him out of there and sent for the "boys" to come and deal with the snake. Luckily the python was well fed and found a nice warm spot to have his siesta…my brother might have been a tasty morsel.

Returning to Malindi was quite an eye opener, and a great disappointment. We stayed at the Eden Rock hotel, but where my parents' shop used to be was now the local Hertz Rentals. It was much scruffier than I remembered and the beach was so sad: it was filthy dirty and covered in seaweed, and the water was impossible to swim in. The River Galana flowed into Malindi and the River Tana flowed into the ocean just north of Malindi, both rivers carrying sewage and polluting the area. However, the beach at Watamu, several miles to the south of Malindi, was delightful and reminded me of Malindi in the old days. There were beautiful white sands and lovely warm blue water to bathe in. We spent many afternoons in that idyllic spot.

We had to take a local taxi to Watamu beach, and one day the taxi broke down in the middle of nowhere. We were dressed in beachwear and the temperatures were stifling hot with no shade to be seen: it was unbearable. Horrific thoughts of three English ladies perishing in the heat went through our minds until a friendly local picked us up in his jeep, and took us to our hotel.

We returned to Nairobi via two small planes, from Malindi to Mombasa and then on to Nairobi, we met up with our driver, where with Diana and my aunt, we headed for Limuru where we were leaving my aunt to stay with a cousin, while Diana and I went up to Molo. We took the "new" road down to Naivasha and Nakuru, and stopped at the Stag's Head, which used to be the place to be in Nakuru, but sadly in the last few decades the hotel had gone out of fashion and was now very neglected and dirty. My father was buried in Nakuru: we tried to find the grave but it was impossible to know where it was.

After lunch we set off on the trip up to Molo and the Highlands Hotel. I don't think anyone had touched the roads since we left Kenya in 1962–3. The potholes were enormous and the trip very slow. There used to be a strip of tarmac running through the village, but when we arrived in Molo it was difficult to see any tarmac except the odd bumps of tar that had not worn out. We travelled up past the Taylor's Farm, where our driver's family worked when we were at the Highlands, and on to the Hotel. Enormous gum trees still grew at the bottom of the drive, and the huge pepper tree kept its place on the lawn. What used to be separate wooden buildings for the office, bar and dining room had been rebuilt and was now a single stone building adjoining the dining room. On registering, we were handed our room key, which was exactly the same key fob we had used when I was a child, with the old telephone and PO Box numbers. I asked the management if I could keep the key fob, but they refused, to my disappointment—it would have been such a nice memento. Our room was exactly as it was when we lived there, except the walls were plastered and painted rather than the rough stone, but the fireplace was blazing, and it was very cosy. Every bedroom had a fireplace, as the evenings were very chilly at 10,000ft.

Dinner that night was a disappointment; the food was not up to the standard my mother had set when she ran the place. The following morning we opened the garden door to find all the horses sleeping or grazing on the lawn in front of us: my mother would have been furious, as the horse's hooves made such a mess of the soft ground.

Diana and I hired two horses and a *syce* (groom) and went out for a lovely ride over the golf course. I could not believe how after 27 years the same paths I used to ride on were still there. We rode up past what had once been the highest tee in the British Empire to the top of the hill 11,000ft and down the other side to the Crosskill's farm and up towards Ballyvistea, where my best friend Bella Ryan used to live. It was a very nostalgic journey for me: as we visited the Keighley's farm on the way back I almost expected June to come out of the house and offer us a cold drink.

On the way back to Nairobi, we went via my first school in Molo, and made ourselves known. I was invited to sign the visitor's book, and we were taken on a tour of the school. There were the first

Bar and Office, Highlands Hotel, Molo, 1960

Bar and office, Highlands Hotel, 1989

Our house, Highlands Hotel, 1960

Looking out towards golf course, our house on right, 1989

Fifi, Jamie Ryan, James Maberley, Charles Keighley, Liz
Ryan, 1960

Anna, just returned from school on horseback 1960

three classrooms, which is all the school consisted of when I first went there, and now it was a Primary and Senior School, and had a reputation of being the second best in Kenya. I felt very proud that this where I started my education.

I asked our driver if he could take us to the Anglican Church which I attended as a child. It was a beautiful building built by Bella's grandfather, Edward Noel Millington (familiarly known as Chub), about 1924. Apparently the first church service was held at the railway station in 1921, but this was very noisy. The church was like a mock Tudor barn, built on land provided by the government and constructed of local red bricks and cedar frames, with a shingle roof supported by Elgon Olive beams. It was like time had stood still: nothing seemed to have changed. Perhaps the trees were larger, but it was still the peaceful church on the hill.

Continuing back to Limuru to pick up my aunt, I asked our driver if he would take us on the escarpment road. He was horrified and said no one used that now except all the heavy lorries. Well, I still wanted to see it again: when I was growing up it had been the only road to Nairobi, and it had the most spectacular views over the Rift Valley. Half way up in a small niche was the smallest church I have ever seen, built by Italian POWs during the 1st World War. The road was worse than I had ever seen; the potholes were so large it was a wonder any vehicle using this road had any suspension left. There was a solid line of lorries travelling up through the dust on the escarpment and the same coming down, and every vehicle moving very slowly trying to negotiate the huge potholes. As travelling was so slow, I didn't suggest that we stop at the church to have a closer look; I did not want to be too late meeting up with Lois, as we still had to travel on into Nairobi, hopefully before dark. As Kenya is on the Equator, there are twelve hours of darkness and twelve hours of daylight, 6 a.m. until 6 p.m., varying only about six minutes over the course of the year. Roughly at 6pm any day of the year it is dark.

***

My great-grandfather came out to Kenya in 1902 to find out more about this new country, leaving his wife and four children in England. When his wife died in England, he arranged for his two older sons to come out to Kenya, and two years later his daughter and youngest son came by ship through the Suez Canal. Sadly his daughter died in Aden and his youngest son (aged 14) had to make arrangements for her to be buried there. There was no way of letting his family know that she had died, as the mail travelled on the same boat he was on. It was his youngest son, Rex Fawcus, who eventually married my grandmother, who had come out to Africa in 1910 as governess to a young girl, Beryl Clutterbuck (Markham), who in later life wrote *West with the Night* and *Straight on Till Morning*. She was the first woman to fly solo from East to West across the Atlantic, and also bred and raced horses in Kenya.

My grandmother, who considered herself a very attractive young lady and definitely felt she should have come from aristocracy, became pregnant; it was assumed by Sir Charles Clutterbuck, Beryl's father. Rex Fawcus, who had grown up and become a local farmer, married my grandmother to give the child a name, Evelyn Reginald Fawcus, and they went on to have two more children, my aunt, Lois, and my mother, Peggy.

Grandmother left Africa and returned to England, finding the climate too hot, the country uncivilized, and I don't think she really liked my grandfather, leaving her three children in Africa with their father. As a young adult, my aunt Lois went to live in England: she married and had three children, David, Penny and Priscilla, before the war, and my cousin James after the war. My uncle Reg, whose conception had been the reason for my grandparents' marriage, went to Canada instead of England. He married a lady from Baltimore, but they never had any children.

My father, James Campbell Murray, was Scottish, and after leaving Glenalmond Public School he joined the Black Watch: he

Grandma, Violet Fawcus, 1910

Grandma (Violet Fawcus) and Evelyn 1913

Grandma (Violet Fawcus) 1918

Lois, Evelyn and Peggy (Mum) 1920

Car loaded for the journey

Arriving in Cape Town, Table Mountain

Mum's trip to Cape, 1949

became an officer and was stationed in British East Africa with the Kenya African Rifles during the first World War with his best friend, Dudley Walsh, protecting the country against German East Africa (Tanganyika). He fell in love with the country, so much so that after the war he decided to go back and settle there in 1924. Before coming back to Kenya he took his friend Dudley home to meet his family, and Dudley eventually married his sister Madge. My father was her favourite brother, and she persuaded Dudley to go out to Kenya in 1946 after the Second World War. My father met his first wife, Kirstie Gillespie, while he was working to build up a coffee estate, and their daughter Kirsten Maureen (Mo) was born in 1930. Kirstie eventually left my father for a man named Phil Chambers, who was helping to build up the coffee estate, and who eventually became the Deputy Director of Agriculture.

Having been in the army during the first World War, my father joined the Air Force when the second World War began. During that time met his second wife, Margot, who was also in the Air Force. They married Kenya in 1939, and were posted to Cairo and then Jerusalem, where my half-sister Diana was born in 1940. After the war, they returned to Kenya.

My mother Peggy stayed on in Africa and lived with her father, only going back to the UK during the war to sign up in the ATS. She returned to Kenya after the war and settled in Malindi with her father.

In May 1949 my mother and her cousin Elizabeth Lindsay, motored 8,500 miles from Kenya to Cape Town. These are her notes she typed on her portable typewriter on the trip.

KITALE to CAPE TOWN
1949

In these days of lightening travel it is rather refreshing to set off on a long safari with time and route being no object: just wandering from place to place as the spirit moves one.

Having fixed the date of departure for sometime at the end of March, the next thing was to prepare the small Morris, Matilda, for the trip. Endless formalities of licences, export permits, insurance and passports had to be tackled, spare parts collected to meet every eventuality, as well as extra petrol and many other details.

The great day dawned and Matilda was duly packed with all the necessary baggage, tennis and squash rackets, and fishing tackle, and at last we were off, from Endebess on the slopes of Mount Elgon.

Practically the whole of the first day was spent circling Mount Elgon, crossing into Uganda near Tororo. Although the next part of the journey was unbearably, hot the road to Jinja was good, and the country lusciously green (due to frequent thunderstorms round Lake Victoria), all the way to Kampala, one of the most attractive towns in East Africa, being built on seven hills. Entebbe, with its beautiful gardens and a wonderful variety of trees and birds, is only a short run from here, right down on the edge of Lake Victoria.

We were struck by the apparent wealth of the natives in Uganda: they are all so well clad and many of them are the proud possessors of bicycles. Cotton and sugar seem to be their chief source of income. At Fort Portal we ran into the first of the season's heavy rains, at one moment almost having to stop as the end of the bonnet was invisible in the deluge. Fort Portal is a small town on the east side of the Ruwenzori Range, the top of which is almost perpetually shrouded in cloud. Disappointed, but not surprised, we had no view of the peaks, although two days later on the west side we were favoured with a crystal clear day and the most beautiful view of the snow capped mountain peaks of the Mountains of the Moon, as they are so romantically named.

It was from Fort Portal that we had our first view of the pyg-mies, down a very lovely escarpment round the north end of the moun-tains; then up over the Buranga Pass from the top of which one gets a wonderful view north—right up to Lake Albert and west—across the low-lying thick tropical forests of the Congo. The descent into the forest was very steep, and the steam from some hot springs was visible from quite a distance. It was not until we were deep into the forest, where the atmosphere is really humid and damp, that we saw the pygmies—a truly amazing race of little people, practically all of them so pot-bellied you wonder how they can ever keep their balance.

The first sight of game was approaching Katwe, where buffalo roam about in great numbers. From the Rest Camp, perched up about 1000 feet above Lake Edward and the plains, one can get a good bird's eye view of elephant, buffalo, water buck and other species, and hippo by the score. Soon after crossing the border into the Congo we were surprised by a flat, wet, muddy hippo getting up practically in front of the car and lurching off at quite a pace. It was not until we reached the Albert National Park that we saw game in any profu-sion, but here with all kinds of animals around us we had our first real thrill. Having taken a number of snaps we were anxious to take a picture of a fairly large elephant who crossed the track just ahead of us, we slowed up alongside and were about to snap him when he swung round as though on a pivot, and amidst great flapping of ears and loud trumpeting made straight for us at great speed. For one breathless second the wheels of the car spun around in the mud before Matilda decided that discretion was the better part of valour, and shot ahead. It was several minutes before we dared breathe easily—great sighs were heaved, and it was longer still before knees stopped quak-ing. It was on this occasion we first appreciated the bottle of brandy brought along purely for medicinal purposes!

All through the mountains round Lake Edward what struck us most was the methodical farming: every hillside was cultivated right to the summit, the contouring a wonderful example of soil conserva-tion. The lakes in the Congo certainly came up to our expectations of splendor. Lake Kivu, with the most attractive holiday resort of

*Kisenyi, boasted a beautiful sandy beach and good sailing in the
most perfect setting under the mountain. Across the north end of the
lake, the road crosses the lava flow from the Nyamlagura Volcano
down to the lake, looking for all the world as if a giant had bulldozed
his way from the lakeside right up to the top of the mountain. There
were many distinct flows running side by side down the mountain, the
most recent being a little over a year old: the top surface was very
brittle and crumbled underfoot, the next flow which had begun to
disintegrate and so on through various stages of growth; first of all a
few rather desolate shoots of bracken, then a little sparse grass until
finally the bush and scrub were quite thick. The next hundred and fifty
miles down the west side of Lake Kivu to Costermansville was one of
the most beautiful runs of the whole trip. The road winding in and out
of the mountains, sometimes climbing hundreds of feet (but always
when one least expected it), with the most exquisite views of the lake
and its many little islands seemingly dotted around at random. On
seventy five miles of this road through the mountains only one-way
traffic is allowed, working each direction on alternate days. We were
fortunate here: as we arrived at the foot of the pass we found it was
the day for us to proceed, for previously we had been quite unaware
of this restriction.*

*Costermansville is a very lovely town, well spread out around
the south end of Lake Kivu, with pleasantly designed modern houses,
all so fresh and clean. The main street runs at right angles to and with
no view of the Lake, and it is here that most of the hotels seem to be
situated. With wonderful visions of a comfortable room in a luxurious
hotel on the water's edge, we were somewhat shattered to find only
one hotel anywhere near the water and all the hotels quite full up; but
we did eventually find a very fifth-rate hotel offering a very small cell
of a room with only the bare necessities and none too clean, overlooking a back yard, a junk heap, and a high wall. Depression set in si-
multaneously with a very heavy thunderstorm: the depression was not
lifted the next morning when the bank refused to cash our traveller's
cheques, which by some unfortunate oversight had not been correctly
stamped. Handbags and pockets were turned out and all remaining*

francs carefully counted; with the aid of higher mathematics it was determined that there were sufficient francs for five more nights. Having intended to spend at least ten more days in the Congo this came as rather a shock. Frantically rushing round doing necessary shopping, packing up and snatching our dripping laundry from out of the hands of the dhobi, we eventually set off with the intention of covering a few miles that day. The road still continued through the mountains; at one or two of the shorter passes we found barriers which were lifted amidst a great beating of drums to notify the native at the other end of the pass there was a car approaching, and so to hold up traffic coming from the other direction. Alas, despite having covered about fifty miles, we came on a barrier with a large sign saying "No traffic may proceed in this direction between sunrise and sunset on Mondays, Wednesday or Friday." It was Friday: retracing our steps a few miles, we found a pleasant clump of trees and camped there until dusk. This caused quite a lot of entertainment to passers-by, as we took this opportunity of drying our still dripping laundry.

These passes were about the most tortuous we had struck, taking us about five and half hours to negotiate seventy miles in the dark: turning up at a gold-mining camp around midnight, we were pleasantly surprised to find the place awake and well-lit, and not in the least surprised to see us.

From then on, for five days of pretty gruelling driving covering twelve hundred miles of flat uncultivated country, we travelled through the copper belt. We negotiated many hair-raising ferries, some of them only a couple of planks laid across dug outs and hauled across the river on a single cable. This country was also typical of Northern Rhodesia, although the ferries were not quite so hazardous.

Good Friday turned out a most unfortunate day for us, with four punctures within about a hundred miles: changing the wheels and mending the puncture in the terrific heat of midday did nothing to ease the situation. At Lusaka, however, luck was with us in that there was a garage open. The walls of the tyres were quite worn out, chiefly due to the shocking state of the roads in Southern Congo, and we had to invest in two new tyres and inner tubes—only to discover later that we had been badly had, as the inner tubes proved to be a size too large and it was not long before these had to be replaced again. On leaving Lusaka we were misdirected and found ourselves on a farm road which obviously had not seen anything more than a bicycle for many moons, climbing up banks over great boulders and potholes large enough to take the whole car: in fact a complete obstacle course for fourteen miles.

After so much monotonous country, the beauty of Victoria Falls was quite intoxicating. They have been so often described, but until one sees them it is impossible to visualize the splendor of these magnificent falls: a mile and a quarter wide crashing down in a deafening thunder nearly four hundred feet into a narrow gorge. The fascination of the complete circular rainbow, the spray rising many feet above the falls and the fairyland of the forest, held us enthralled for many hours. Leaving the car for sometime here, we were greatly amused to find on our return several baboons clambering all over Matilda: luckily the doors and windows were locked, or goodness knows what destruction they might have wrought. There was one young fellow with his mother: he had great difficulty clambering up as he could barely reach the bumper bar and he found everything about the car so slippery to hang on to. Having kept us entertained for some time, we rewarded the baboons with some acid drops and at last, as dusk was approaching, we had to bid them all farewell.

We travelled on south to Bulawayo with its beautiful wide roads, and the rugged beauty of the Matopos Hills, with Rhode's grave on the summit of World's View, the highest of these hills. At Bulawayo we had our first contretemps with the police, who caught us quite inadvertently crossing against the traffic lights (the first we had met on this trip): the young police officer, not being put off his duty by two girls who could not take the matter seriously, took our Kenya address and warned us that of course we would receive a caution. Somehow, I don't think he knew Kenya!

The trip through Salisbury up into the highlands of Southern Rhodesia was quite uneventful. Inyanga and Umtali are really *quite beautiful: here we spent four days winding our way through the mountains. From Umtali we climbed up into the Vumba Hills: as it was nearly dark on leaving Umtali, we had some good views of the lights of the town, getting more and more distant until the final view we had of them, hundreds of feet below the road was just a fairyland of twinkling lights in the far distance. Very loathe we were to leave the mountains once more, for Fort Victoria and the Zimbabwe Ruins: very little seems to be known of the latter, but we were much impressed with the height and solidity of some of the walls, and only wished to learn more of the history of this stronghold.*

After once getting used to the tarmac strips in Southern Rhodesia, the roads are comparatively good. On passing through Beit Bridge, another chapter of our trip seemed to be over, and so into the Union. The first night was spent up in the hills overlooking Louis Trichardt: here, on the following day, we encountered one of their torrential hail storms; for several hours after the storm we kept coming across drifts of hail along the road, sometimes over a foot deep. We followed the Northern section of the Drakensbergs down the east side to Graskop and Pilgrims Rest, where we found the roads appalling— at one point we had to get out and give Matilda a push, through mud almost axle deep.

It was a great disappointment to find the Kruger national Park closed, although Pretorius Kop at the south end is open all year round; so hoping to see some lion we made our way there, only to strike unlucky once more. Either we did not go to the right spot or we missed them in the long grass, but we saw none; apart from some fine greater kudu and wildebeest and buck of various kinds we saw very little.

Nearing Pretoria we really felt that we were approaching civilsation again. We spent several days there, and were fortunate to be there on the first Saturday of the month when their magnificent Union Buildings are floodlit: this is a wonderful sight. We were completely overawed by the hustle and bustle of Johannesburg, but found the one advantage being the E.A.(K) number plate, which got us out of all sorts of parking difficulties. After parking on taxi ranks, loading bays and various other prohibited places, we only received kind warnings and advice for future occasions. The relief of getting away from the swift tempo of the city was great, especially as it was not long before we got up into the mountains again. Having left Durban and the very lovely Valley Thousand Hills behind us, we retraced our steps to Bergville. Here again we encountered a very heavy storm, and on trying to reach Cathedral Peak where we intended to spend the night, were completely bogged down. Happily there was a lull in the storm and although it was night and our only torch had failed, the continuous lightening came to our assistance, making it as bright as daylight. After a great tussle we donned chains and extricated ourselves, although not before being covered with mud from head to foot. We then decided the evil you know is better than the evil you don't know, so made our way back to Bergville. On waking the next morning we were greeted with the reflection of the rising sun on the majestic splendor of the snow-capped Drakensberg range.

Unfortunately by this time we just becoming conscious of the passage of time, and could not spend nearly as long as we would have wished exploring the mountains, although we did spend one day wandering up the mountains and in the Umzikulu Valley before making our way through Kokstad to Queenstown and the Katberg Pass. The next port of call was Port Elizabeth, and here, had it not been for the bitter cold, we would most certainly have taken a swim as the surf looked most inviting.

We followed the coast road down to Plettenberg Bay, with its attractive hotel on an island, thence to Knysna and its Stinkwood Forests, down through deep gorges and up through one of the most lovely passes, Prince Alfred's Pass to Outshoorn and the Cango Caves. These are an incredible sight and the lighting effects on the stalagmites and stalactites are a work of art. Fairyland, Little Switzerland and the Devil's Workshop are only a few of the many very aptly named caves. It was quite a pantomime watching the sightseers of all shapes and sizes tussling their way through and up some of the very low, narrow tunnels.

Not far from here the Zwartberg Mountains rise up in their splendor, with the Zwartberg Pass over to Prince Albert and the edge of the Great Karoo. The vast splendor of the view is only surpassed by the awe-inspiring mountains and gorges through which the road crept. Just to prove the prowess of Matilda—and much to the amazement of many of the larger limousines—we negotiated the pass twice. Although this entailed a lot of first-gear work and boiling in the radiator, Matilda sailed up without any apparent effort. Matters were complicated a little, though, by getting a puncture on the way down; with the aid of a few odd boulders under the wheels we changed the wheel without mishap.

So, we made our way through all the ostrich farms to Calitzdorp and Swellendam down to Hermanus, a lovely spot on the coast. Here we spent a couple of days before the last lap of the journey to Cape Town, over Sir Lowry's Pass, from where we had a first view of Table Mountain and so to Cape Town and, alas, the end of a perfect safari.

***

Over the course of eight weeks they toured Uganda, the Belgian Congo, Northern and Southern Rhodesia and most of South Africa, finally arriving in Cape Town. They carried a revolver for protection, but apart from six tyre punctures (which they repaired themselves), they had no mishaps. Among highlights of their trip were visits to the pygmies who live at the foot of the Ruwenzori Mountains (The Mountains of the Moon) in the Northern Congo, an erupting volcano called Nyamlaguria on Lake Kivu, and the Albert National Game Park, where they narrowly escaped a charging bull elephant. They had to cut short their trip through the Congo as they ran out of francs, and spent three dinnerless nights during their dash for the Rhodesian border, as they didn't have money to pay for food.

My mother returned to Malindi where she met my father. I have little information about how my father and his second marriage ended: Diana only remembers returning from boarding school for the Easter holidays to find her father was no longer living at home. My parents must have met about that time, as I would have been conceived around Easter. When I was about 25 years old, I learnt that my parents married after I was born, and it made my getting a passport difficult. Their marriage certificate was torn on the year of the marriage: the damage had been sellotaped and "March 1950" written across the date. The authorities would not accept this, so I had to apply for a new one, which showed they were married in March 1951. I presume my mother did this to protect us from any sort of gossip; I never found out until ten years after she died.

I was born in Mombasa hospital on Friday the 13th of November, and we lived in Malindi where my father had his *duka*. I remember blissful days walking on the beach with our African *ayah* and my mother telling friends that my brother Andrew and I could swim before we could walk, and that we spoke Swahili before English.

My father was a sickly man, and the climate was too hot on the coast, so we moved up country to the foothills of Kilimanjaro in Tanganyika (now Tanzania), where my mother ran the Lawns Hotel at Lushoto. It was lush and green, and strawberries and bananas grew wild; sisal was the main crop in that area, grown to make string and jute bags, and it was everywhere, and I remember thinking what a boring plant it was.

We were introduced to riding at the Lawns Hotel. My mother, a very keen horsewoman, popped us on ponies at a very young age, and Andrew and I both took to it like ducks to water.

This was during the Emergency of the Mau Mau, and life was very dangerous. The Kikuyu were very agitated and wanted to drive the whites out of Kenya. It is believed their leader was Jomo Kenyatta: he was interned and tried, and found guilty. He was imprisoned in Lodwar in the Northern desert area of Kenya. The Mau Mau, which consisted of the Kikuyu tribe, hid in the forests and around Mt Kenya, coming out at night to slaughter cattle and ransack farms belonging to white families. They left cattle hamstrung and bellowing until their owners found them in the morning, and had to shoot them to put them out of their misery. Whites and many thousands of Africans were

Anna and Andrew, 1952

Murray's Duka, 1950

Anna and Andrew with Ayah, 1952

Andrew and Anna with Ayah, 1953

Anna riding Flicka 1955

Anna and Andrew, 1955

Anna, Mum (Peggy Murray) and Andrew, 1955

Anna, Dad (Campbell Murray) Andrew 1955

Andrew, Anna and Mo, 1955

Lawns Hotel, Lushoto, Tanganyika

Andrew riding Nora, 1955

Dad, (Campbell Murray), Andrew and Anna, 1955

slaughtered with *pangas*, the long big bladed knives used by most farmers and Africans.

One family we knew was listening to the radio and reading the papers, with their children asleep in their beds, when their day workers (who were Kikuyu) came back into their house, tied them up with barbed wire and slashed them with pangas and left them for dead. The wife was killed but the husband and their children survived. Everyone was afraid of these attacks: most houses were built on the ground level with only one floor, and people began installing wooden shutters on their windows to protect their homes and families from the intruders.

My father had to return to UK for various medical reasons, leaving my mother alone during the Emergency with two small children. On one occasion my mother, having had some sort of premonition, moved all her bedroom furniture: she put the wardrobe opposite the window and shifted the bed to the side wall. That evening, there was an attack and shots were fired through the shutters into the wardrobe: they were obviously meant to be for my mother. We survived the Mau Mau, but many of our friends did not—my cousin Nigel Walsh, Dudley Walsh's son, who served in the Kenya Regiment, was shot in the leg; his hip was shattered and he spent six months in hospital. He suffered for five years from shrapnel.

Eventually we had to move up country near a main hospital and doctors. We left Lushoto for Nakuru in the Rift Valley in Kenya, where my father's sister Madge and Dudley Walsh lived with their family. All our worldly belongings were loaded into a lorry and we started our trek into Kenya. It was the rainy season and the lorry kept getting stuck in the mud. The roads were very muddy, narrow and almost impassable, particularly on the hills. My mother unloaded her precious Indian rugs to place under the wheels of the lorry to give it traction: it must have broken her heart to use such valuable rugs. I believe they were rolled up again and sent to the cleaners when we arrived in Nakuru, as I remember the Indian rugs in our homes throughout my childhood.

I was six years old and my father was very ill. My mother was working for an accounting firm at that time, and every day after school my father and I would walk along to her office near the town arboretum to meet her. One day he told me he wasn't feeling well enough and I was to go on my own. I was something of a little princess, and I adored my father: I felt very miffed that my father was not coming, denying me the pleasure of our usual walk. I skipped off to meet my mother, but when I met her I did not pass on the message that my father was not well until we were approaching our house. My mother rushed in, called an ambulance and doctor and my father was carried off to hospital. My father died a few weeks later, and it was several years before I ever forgave myself for not letting my mother know sooner. I was sure that had I not been so pig-headed, he would have lived, and that it was entirely my fault that he died. It wasn't until I was 14 or 15 that I even owned up to this to my mother: she reassured me that his death was nothing to do with me—a few minutes would not have changed the end result. I only knew him for six years of my life, but I still missed him, and do so even to this day. I found out that my father had been married twice before and I had two-half sisters, one by each prior marriage.

After his death, my mother took over the Highlands Hotel in Molo, which was even further up country, very high and out of the Rift Valley. There was a golf course with the highest tee in the British Empire; we had horses, two herds of dairy cattle, Guernseys and Jerseys, sheep, pigs, turkeys, several hundred acres of farmland and a 25-bedroom hotel. My mother was obviously deeply in mourning, but as a child I never noticed.

***

Mwaniki

He's dead I know but
I can hear his bass voice shout 'bafu, bafu!' and
feel the slap, slap of his splayed brown feet,
cracked at the heels, chasing behind me.
I fall into his arms in a breathless mass of laughter.

Childishly bored
I seek him out in the dark back kitchen
where I am not supposed to be but
he won't tell.
I watch the potato peelings fall
from between his pink-palmed hands
and smell the hiss of his spit as he tests the flat iron.
He lets me pattern the pie with a fork
and smooth my father's handkerchiefs.
On an upturned bucket
he lets me dry the knives
under his sharp gaze.
He won't tell.

He's dead I know and it's long ago but
the deep, dark smell of him—
the feel of the loving life of him—
and the sound of the catch of his rough hands on my jersey
as he let me go
are with me here.

* Bafu – Kiswahili for bath

Bella's poem and her memories of her beloved Mwaneki.
My best friend, Isobel (Bella) Ryan, was one of our closest neigh-

bours, seven miles away. We spent a lot of time together—we were
both interested in sewing and knitting, and both our mothers helped
us with sewing projects. My mother, who knitted beautiful fair
isle sweaters taught me the art, and it has given me great pleasure
throughout my life.

Bella's father was the Master of Hounds in Molo and her
brother Pip was a whipper-in. I was first "blooded" at the age of eight.
This seemed a strange ritual to me when I was young, where a child
or perhaps an adult on his or her first hunt had their face smeared
with blood from the hoof of the deer, and it was traditional to leave
it there all day. This is considered an honour in the hunting field and
happened only once for a person, usually the first time a person stayed
with the hunt until the quarry was brought down.

Bella shared some of her memories of my mother with me:

"Your mother in my childhood memory was fiery-tempered,
and yet her ample bosom was literally so soft and comforting to
lean against. Her alto voice brought the comfort of knowing she was
hugely in control of us, the Africans, her life; she seemed scared of
nothing; she drove like a maniac; she had indomitable energy, ideas,
and plans for us; she managed to 'look after us' despite never being
around. I remember entering all the 'shows' with vegetable sculptures,
losing the twin of the Norwegian fair isle jumper she knitted for you
and me (I left it under a bench at a point-to-point); eating jelly whilst
watching *The African Queen* in that long lounge organised by your
mum (the first film I had ever seen) and hearing her come over to the
house to make us put the lights out if I was staying with you.
Strangely, I don't remember her in our house—she was probably
always on duty. I do remember my mother and her together at the
Highlands, though."

We bought the most delicious strawberries, bilberries and raspberries from the Research Station every weekend for the dessert table.
Wild strawberries seemed to grow all year and they remain the most
delicious I have ever tasted. Not having seasons in Kenya made it
quite difficult to grow many things taken for granted in seasonal coun-

tries: certain fruits and flowers could be grown under "false" seasons, and the roses bloomed all year, but we could never grow real daffodils in Kenya. I never saw a daffodil until I was an adult in England. My mother always held a Daffodil Ball at the hotel, but there was not one real daffodil to be seen. She made them all painstakingly by hand, of yellow paper.

My mother yelled, "Anna, have you got all your things for ballet this afternoon? The horses are waiting outside. You had better hurry or you will be late for school." I grabbed my bag with my blue ballet dress, blue knickers, white socks and ballet shoes, and tucked my school dress into my jodhpurs, stuffing my felt school hat into the bag. I kissed my mother goodbye and went out to the horses, where the syce was waiting for me. I handed him my bag, put my foot in the stirrup and popped up onto Rainbow. We walked down the steep drive on the grass verge; our horses were not shod, so we rode on the soft ground. We turned right onto the main road for half a mile, and never saw a car, and then turned left towards the Research Station where the road was murrum, soft enough for the horses' feet.

Passing the Research Station, we then came to the end of the road and took a path into the forest. The trees met overhead and we rode through this tunnel of shade. Now that we were off the road, we trotted for the next half an hour, occasionally breaking into a canter and squinting in the bright light as we emerged from the woods. We passed fields with cattle grazing and a donkey trying to get better things from the hedge on the other side of the fence. Eventually we came out onto the Molo road: there was traffic, but for the most part it was only the odd few cars that always slowed down as they passed us. Half a mile on we turned left into the driveway of the school; I jumped off Rainbow, ran my stirrups up and passed the reins to the syce. I took the bag he had been carrying and thanked him and said I would see him at 5 p.m. I ran into school, pulling my dress out of my jodhpurs and into the girls' changing rooms. I whipped off my jodhs and hung my bag with ballet things and riding hat on my peg, just as the bell rang for Assembly.

Being on the Equator, we were not allowed outside to play at break time or lunch if we did not have our felt hats with us. We were also supposed to arrive and leave wearing our hats, but as I often had two hats, I was excused. Every day after lunch, we had to rest for half an hour. Each of us had a mattress and rug and we would take them outside under the trees and rest or sleep or chat quietly or play naughts and crosses, so long as we didn't get up and run around or talk too loudly.

When school finished in the afternoon, if we had ballet as I did on Tuesdays, we went over to the hostel where we had tea and then had to change and have our ballet lesson. Bella and I were the tallest in the ballet class and we were by far the most awkward dancers, but we had such fun when they held performances and we had to learn a piece and get all dressed up and dance with our partners. One year I was Katie Kangaroo and Bella was Dilly Duck; we were never the pixies or fairy queens.

After the lesson, I would quickly pull on my jodhs, tucking my ballet dress into them, stuffing my hat and school dress into the bag and handing it to the *syce*, while I got back onto Rainbow. We could not dilly-dally on the way home, as darkness came sharp at 6 p.m.: we went up onto the road then turned off by the fields and into the forest. It seemed much darker now, but I felt very safe having the *syce* with me, and we trotted most of the way. We arrived back at the Highlands at 5.45pm and at the office I dismounted and handed the reins to the syce and ran the stirrups up.

My mother usually came out to greet us with, "How was your day, Darling? Did they tell you what parts you were playing in the ballet? Why don't you take your things over to the house and then come and have supper? I will wait for you here."

For me, life was idyllic. Some days I would ride to school and back on my pony Rainbow, arriving back at the hotel in time for tea. Mum would be waiting for me and we would sit on the verandah or choose from the sumptuous display of cakes, scones and sandwiches in the lounge. On other days Mrs. Ryan would collect Bella and me from school, or my Mother would pick us up and we would all have tea on the verandah. I remember many times spending the night at the Ryans' after school, or Bella staying with us. We had such different homes: I grew up in the hotel, she lived in a regular family home on the farm. At six o'clock Mwaniki would light the fires in all the rooms and also the Tilley lamps. He would run a bath and Bella, Jamie, her younger brother, and I would all get it and splash around until we were told to get out and get ready for supper. Bella, Jamie and I would then have supper, prepared by Mwaniki. My favourites were cheese dream, which was cheese on toast or in the US, grilled cheese, and another was baked eggs with HP sauce. After supper we would join the rest of the family around the fire in the sitting room. Before going to bed, we would all kneel down in the sitting room and say our prayers, asking God to bless all the Ryans and the Murrays.

When Bella stayed with me, we might often go for a ride on the golf course and then come in for supper in the main dining room at 6 o'clock. We had electricity from a generator, which came on at 6pm and was switched off at midnight, but all the fires had been lit as it became very chilly when the sun went down. After supper we would go over to our house and have a bath and sit round the fire in the sitting room, while my mother read us a story. It was a very comforting, cosy childhood. Our beds were always turned down with a hot water bottle, and the fire lit in the bedroom. I remember longing to have a normal home and making my own bed, but when I did, I came home to find it had been remade properly.

It was fun to go to the *dobi* (laundry). Behind the ironing room was a paddock with lots of tin baths in it, and they were filled up with washing, mostly whites and a few coloured washes in the baths. I often wondered how they could get all the sheets and tablecloths so white in our muddy murrum water, but a lot of "blue" was used to whiten the wash. The Africans would roll up their trousers and tramp the washing clean, and then everything would be hung out on the lines in the paddock. The smell in the ironing room is something that I will always remember; the irons were filled with charcoal and left to get to the right temperature to iron all the sheets, pillow cases and tablecloths. It was a heavenly smell of charcoal and ironed linens, so fresh and fragrant.

My mother always hand washed our sweaters, rather than send them to the laundry, and she would dry them on towels on the lawn outside our house. The garden was totally secluded with a high thuyer hedge, and she always felt it was safe to leave them there to dry. Andrew and I both had beautiful matching fair isle sweaters she had knitted, and she washed my brother's and left it on the lawn, but it disappeared.

Several months later when I was playing up near the African *Boma* (this was an area where the Africans lived and had a wooden shanty fence around it) I saw Andrew's sweater on a small *toto* (child). I ran home and told my mother I had seen Andrew's sweater on a *toto,* and she went up to the *Boma* and retrieved it. Unfortunately it was so dirty, worn and misshapen my mother decided to throw it out. We had a lot of problems with light fingers in Kenya and it was never a good idea to leave anything lying around.

I remember for my tenth birthday, with the rust-coloured jeans my mother gave me, she also gave me my first watch. I was so proud of having a watch for the first time and treasured it. At the pony club during the Christmas holidays, we went out for a hack in the afternoon and I knew I was doing wrong but I just loved the new shoes my mother had bought me. They were slip-ons with a leather ruff across the instep. There were two rules about riding that my mother was completely adamant about and that was, that we wore a riding hat and wore the right shoes or boots. They had to be leather with a heel and no fussy bits to catch on stirrups. On this afternoon I chose to wear my new shoes and when we came to the first ditch a young boy fell off, and as I was behind him, I got off to help him on again. When I went to get back on my horse, everyone else had moved off and I had my foot in the stirrup and my horse moved off too. I couldn't get my foot out of the stirrup because of the leather ruff on the instep and I was dragged and when I put my hand down on the ground I broke my wrist.

I was helped back on the horse and one of the adults came back to the stables with me and then drove me home to my mother. Instead of sympathy, my mother was furious to find I was wearing my new shoes instead of sensible riding shoes. I was sitting in the bathroom at home and my mother was looking at my wrist and took my watch off and put it on the bathroom window sill, and then decided she would need to take me to Nakuru to get it X-rayed and plastered up. Nakuru was two hours' drive away, so she was not too happy, and on our return, I went to get my watch and found it had been stolen from the window sill.

One day my mother asked me if I wanted to ride with some guests from the hotel, so I changed and joined everyone in front of the office, where the horses had been brought down from the stables. I saw my favourite horse Dolly there, and asked my mother if I could ride her, but she said no, I was to ride Piccadilly. I rolled my eyes, but sighed and agreed. We rode out between the thuyer hedges onto the golf course and turned up the hill and rode on the edge of the fairway until we came to the highest tee, then we took a path to the very top of the hill.

"Can we stop a moment please? This horse is too much of a handful for me. I think I will just walk back leading it." The guest riding Dolly pleaded.

"Oh, no problem," I said. "I will ride Dolly and you can have Piccadilly."

So we swopped horses, and no sooner had we all settled down to come back down the hill when Dolly took off at a gallop, straight down the fairway. She was going so fast she nearly collided with the gate at the entrance to the thuyer hedges, but it caught my leg and knocked me off at full gallop. My mother heard my screams from the office and came out just as Dolly galloped past her. She ran down through the hedges to find me in a heap, in agony and unable to get up. My mother carried me to the office and brought the car around to take me to the doctor. Thankfully nothing was broken, but my calf muscle was damaged and I could not put my foot to the ground for weeks. I was on crutches for a while, and again my mother was very displeased with me for changing horses. She told me Dolly was far too strong for any child to ride, and only let me ride her in the ring.

My brother was sent off to prep school as a boarder, absent from our lives for 13 weeks at a time. I remember the trips up to Kitale, where Andrew went to school; as we crossed the Equator, there was a bridge that crossed the railway and we often used to stop, especially if a diesel train was passing. We could hear it in the distance and see the white smoke and smell the diesel as it chuffed up the hill. As we crossed the bridge we would all chant, "We are south of the Equator, we are south of the Equator, now we are north of the Equator, we are north of the Equator!" It was a ritual we did every time we passed over this bridge.

Only much later, when we were adults, did I learn how affected Andrew was by this life—he said he didn't know his parents at all, which was so true.

During the holidays, there was always a pony club camp, and both Andrew and I attended it. We camped in tents near the tennis club and stabled our horses in the polo stables: the riding classes were held on the Polo field. In the afternoons we went for a ride or had the opportunity to jump over the point-to-point jumps. This was very exciting as they were huge, about four feet high, but usually brush so our small ponies could scramble over them. These camps were the highlight of our holidays, and always ended with a competition, like a three-day event, except it was all done in one day, and at three different levels. There was dressage, cross-country and show jumping.

At school we were putting on the production of "Robin Hood" as a pageant in the school grounds. I was a senior, but I was absolutely not an actor. Robin Hood and his Merry Men rode in on horses. Our horses were used, so I was given the part of Much; when everyone got off their horses to play their parts, I jumped off and took all the horses from the actors.

The previous week my mother had bought a new chestnut and I rode him. When I jumped off and rushed forward leading the chestnut, to take Jester who was ahead of me, Jester lashed out at my horse

1956 Back: Dad, Madge, Sheila Knox, Kathleen, Nigel Walsh Middle: Sheila Walsh, Brenda Walsh, Adrian Walsh, Dudley
Walsh, Anna, Fiona Knox, Andrew Murray, Donald Knox and Ian Knox

1960 Back: Richard F, Mum, Dudley Walsh, Pauline F, Nigel F, Michael F Middle: Linnet F, John F, Susan F, Carolyn F, Eileen F, Gina F, Centre: Joan F and Great Aunt Xandra F Bott:om: Jenny F, Xandra F, Anna, Ronald F, Andrew Murray

but caught me in the stomach. He was a big horse with feet as wide as soup plates. There was total mayhem, and I was badly hurt. I was carried to the sick bay and a doctor was called: I couldn't straighten my body and had to remain curled up. Fortunately he caught me in the stomach and no bones were broken, but for weeks I had an enormous black bruise in the shape of Jester's hoof, and it was several days before I could stand up straight.

The day after the pageant my mother had planned to take us on our first safari to the Queen Elizabeth National Park in Uganda. I was so excited about the safari that I told my mother I was fine, despite being unable to stand up and having to move around doubled up. She decided to risk taking me, as we had miles of driving and there was no harm in me sitting in the car. We stayed in very basic accommodation, consisting of a hut-like structure with four fold-up canvas beds as the only furniture. There was a kitchen hut with a stove and a sink, which all other visitors used as well. Also some distance away was the washroom, which consisted of a loo and basin with cold water.

After a supper of baked beans and tinned sausages, I needed to go to the loo before bed and my mother suggested that I pop outside behind our hut and spend a penny, as there were no lights and we had one lamp. I went outside in my nightdress and squatted down in the dark and suddenly there was a terrible noise of laughter or a cackle. I rushed back inside, frightened because the noise had sounded so close; my mother assured me it was nothing to worry about and the hyena was probably much further off than it seemed.

The following morning we went off in search of animals and headed up to the Ruwenzories, where we came across pygmies on the side of the road; they were rolling a woven basket that was about ten feet high and five feet in diameter. I could not imagine what such small people were going to do with a basket of that size. As we travelled on into the mountains we came across the rare sight of three gorillas crossing the road.

As a child I never felt deprived, poor or lacking in anything. I remember before Christmas a huge parcel would arrive from England from my aunt Lois. It would be full of the most gorgeous clothes I had ever set eyes on, plus parcels wrapped for Christmas for each of us. I remember one year getting a beautiful red dress that I wore until it was far too small for me, and my mother almost had to tear it off me. I don't remember my mother ever buying me clothes, and yet I always had plenty. She knitted us the most beautiful fair isle jerseys, often making matching ones for Bella and me. If I ever needed special costumes for my ballet she always made them, and I remember her making me a very smart riding jacket for shows. I do remember her buying me a pair of rust-coloured jeans for my tenth birthday, and I was very proud of them, but somehow most of my clothes seemed to come from England and a few were passed on from cousins.

Christmas day was a very exciting time. After church at 10 a.m., all the relations would come to us, as we had the space to cater for a large family get together and my mother couldn't leave the hotel anyway. It was always such fun waiting for everyone to arrive, the anticipation of seeing cousins we hadn't seen for a while. As soon as Jenny and Xandra arrived, we three girls rushed off down the garden and climbed the old gum tree that had been chopped down many moons ago before left as a climbing apparatus for children to play on. We hadn't seen each other in many months and chatted and laughed until my mother called us to come and join the family for a drink before lunch. Dear Great aunt Xandra caught my attention and in her special deep voice asked me how I was doing at school. We chatted for a while before we were called into the dining room for lunch. What a sight would meet our eyes! The table was laden with the most delicious goodies, always the same every year. Down the centre of the table were naatchies (tangerines) and various nuts in the shells and nutcrackers beside them. Scattered on the white tablecloth were Quality Street sweets and in front of each place setting and criss-crossed round the table were crackers. This was our traditional Christmas table. While we were waiting for the turkey to be brought out, we pulled the crackers and put on the silly hats and read the jokes, and hunted for the surprise in each cracker. It would either be a key ring, a miniature pack of cards, a magic trick, or something small and pretty useless, but it would always be so exciting to see what everyone got.

My mother would carve the turkey and the vegetables and roast potatoes with piggies in the blanket (sausages wrapped in bacon) turkey stuffing, bread sauce, cranberry sauce, and gravy would all be handed round for us to help ourselves. Seconds were always offered and those of us who had room would take a second helping. At this stage there was always a pause before the Christmas pudding was brought out. Presents were exchanged with a lot of excitement and wrapping paper everywhere. Once all the paper and leftover crackers, nut shells, tangerine skins, and sweet papers had all been cleared, my mother came in with the pièce de résistance, a huge Christmas pudding aflame. She would serve out the pudding and pass the plates around and we would all add brandy butter or cream. My mother kept up the old tradition of hiding a sixpence in the pudding, and there was always great excitement to see who got it. For those who didn't want Christmas pudding, individual mince pies were also handed around.

After we had finished with coffee and liqueurs for the adults, my mother suggested we sit on the steps outside the dining room for a family photo, followed by a walk on the golf course. All of us children romped and ran, while the adults and older teenagers were far more sedate. Everyone took care of Great aunt Xandra, my grandfather's brother's wife—she was fairly elderly, and a remarkable woman who left her mark on Kenya history. aunt Xandra was a great friend of Alice, Duchess of Gloucester, and between them they did so much to establish the East African Women's League (EAWL) in Kenya. She was the Chairman for many years in Kenya and the UK, and she was also involved in the Country Women of the World.

***

There was talk about Kenya getting its independence and people were getting worried, not knowing what would happen once Kenyatta became President on his release from prison. This was a man everyone had feared during the early 1950s, and now he was being freed and would take over from the British. My mother sacked her Kikuyu employees, as she was afraid of trouble. It was a sad day, as two of her *pishis* (cooks) were Kikuyu; they had always seemed very faithful, but she did not trust them now that Jomo Kenyatta was coming into power.

Kenya gained independence in 1963 and my mother, and all other non-Africans, tried to get what they could out of the country. All British subjects had to become Kenya citizens or leave the country, and my mother wanted to keep her British passport. In December 1962 I had taken the KPE (Kenya Preliminary Examination) and was due to move up to high school in January: originally I was registered to go to Eldoret Highlands, which was not too far from my brother's prep school in Kitale, but with Independence on the horizon my mother decided to send me ahead to South Africa so I could start school at the beginning of the school year there (in Kenya and South Africa the school year runs from January to December). My mother had to stay on in Kenya to sell up and sort out her affairs before leaving for South Africa, and Andrew stayed on at his prep school.

In January 1963 we set off for Mombasa in our little Austin A40. It was a hot and dusty trip. Coming out of Nairobi we saw giraffes and zebra grazing as we passed the Nairobi National Park. There were herds of wildebeest and also some gazelle and dik dik. The road was dusty with lorries loaded to overflowing with pineapples, and others carrying sisal and various wares, all heading for the markets in Nairobi. On the side of the road we saw *mukati* shacks (mukati means made with banana leaves) with Africans selling fruit, and we stopped for some mangos. We passed a rickety old bus laden with people, chickens, boxes tied on with string and a poor goat standing on the roof and tied there to stop it falling off.

Eventually we arrived at Voi and pulled in to the Voi Hotel, where we stayed the night. It was very hot and our beds had mosquito nets, which were all pulled out over the beds by the time we had had dinner. We rose early the next morning and had a quick breakfast before continuing our trip to Mombasa. I was becoming more apprehensive as we neared our destination, but it was also exciting. I had never been on a ship before, but the thought of leaving my mother and brother made me feel very sad. I hoped the family I was travelling with were nice; we had never met them, although my mother had communicated by letter and phone.

As we neared Mombasa, the landscape changed from arid and dusty with red soil and the odd thorn trees to a lighter brown soil with more leafy trees—banana, palm, mango and baobab trees, which had huge wide trunks and branches ending up as twigs, but no greenery on them. As we entered Mombasa we passed through the enormous elephant tusks planted on either side of the road, like a gateway into the city. We were struck by the hubbub and noise of people bustling on foot and on bikes, the stench of hot bodies mingled with the smell of the sea, and masses of cars trying to get from one place to another. Eventually my mother made her way to the docks where we saw the "Africa." She was so large and I couldn't believe that I was going to sail in her.

Somehow we managed to meet up with the Dawson family, with whom I was going to travel. Mrs. Dawson seemed very nice and her four sons were aged from four to twelve. My mother and brother came up on deck and we found the cabin I was to share with the Dawsons: we returned to the deck to say our sad farewells, and they left the boat with many others who had come on board to say goodbye. They stood on the dock waving as the ship left its moorings.

I didn't have time to be very sad: there was so much to do on the ship, and as we passed Beira the seas were so rough, we were taken to our beds with sea sickness. Eventually all was calm and we sailed into Durban where I was to meet my half-sister Mo and brother-in-law Bert.

CHAPTER 2

SOUTH AFRICA

I was met at the docks in Durban by my half-sister Mo and her husband Bert. I remember meeting her once or twice before in my life, but I couldn't say I really knew her.

South Africa was very exciting. There were more cars than I had ever seen, double-decker buses, traffic lights, tea-rooms, public swimming pools, tarred roads, electricity all day, ice cream vans and clear rather than muddy water that didn't need to be filtered for drinking. All these new things made it seem like stepping into a new world.

In Kenya my mother had a fine reputation at the Highlands Hotel for the marvelous food, and people came for miles to eat there. I wanted to follow in her footsteps and go into the hotel and catering trade, but it wasn't so easy in South Africa and it was decided that once I left school I would go to England to study. For now, though, I was about to begin school in South Africa.

We had a few weeks before I started at my new school, Pietermaritzburg Girl's High. The school clothes list seemed very long and included six pairs of knickers and six pairs of knicker liners. I wondered what knicker liners were until we went to the school outfitters and found that knickers were bloomers with elastic legs and knicker liners were normal underwear: I was informed that one wore the bloomers over the knicker liners. I could not believe that we were expected to wear two pairs of underwear, but I soon found out that it was advisable to do as we were told. I came to school one day wearing my normal underwear, and we had gym in the second period. We had to strip down to the square necked shirts we wore and knickers. Everyone was wearing the regulation green knickers except me, and our gym mistress made me do gym in my ordinary underwear and also gave me an order mark for not obeying the rules. I was humiliated, and I never forgot to wear my knickers, especially on sports days, which were most school days.

1963 - Sue Phillips and me enjoying all the new exciting things in South Africa, before my mother arrived

1963 - Sue Phillips and me bumper boating in Durban

1963 - Sue Phillips and me taking a rickshaw ride in Durban

1963 - Sherry and me, one of the first ponies my mother bought us when she arrived in South Africa

In the few weeks before school started, Mo and I sewed nametapes on every possible item that could be marked, and in my spare time I became really enthused in making model planes, ships and cars. I could not resist spending every penny of my pocket money on models and I lined my room with them. It was all such a new experience, and perhaps a strange hobby for a 12-year-old girl.

I was introduced to the ice-cream van that came round honking its melodious horn. Ice cream was a new treat: we never had ice cream in Kenya, as we never had freezers, but here it was the norm for most people to enjoy ice-creams daily. It was very hot in January and so refreshing to sit on the verandah enjoying our ice creams.

Mo took me to a riding school so I could ride again, knowing how much I was missing our horses. I really enjoyed this, as I felt I was having proper tuition, which somehow I rarely had. The horses were always there to ride and my mother used to say, "Sit up, toes in, heels down," but really everything I learned was at Pony Club. Mrs Schall at the riding school let me ride some lovely ponies and she arranged horse shows, which were great fun.

At the end of January, Mo and Bert loaded my trunk and cases into the car and I wore my new school uniform, which was a pale green tunic with square-necked white blouse underneath, finished off with a tan blazer with green and white piping and a white panama hat with green and white ribbon. On arriving at the hostel, I found eight new students, all from Kenya; I knew two of them from my village, Pam Crystal, who was in my class, and Sue Phillips, who was two years ahead of me. As we were all newbies in a foreign country, we tended to stick together and support each other. Pam was the only one in my form—the others were a year ahead. That first term was pretty rough on us all and we took a lot of ragging, leg pulling and teasing because of the way we spoke; one of the girls, Lynn, was nicknamed Pommie or Pom. Not only did we have to put up with that, we had to learn a new language, Afrikaans, which was part of the curriculum. The school laid on extra Afrikaans lessons for us Kenyans after school. These were a real chore and made our days so much longer

Mum, Peggy Murray, 1946

Dad, Campbell Murray, 1946

Lois Ashwanden about 1995

than everyone else's, and I am not sure any of us caught up to the level of our peers in class. It was not like arriving in France and having to speak only French, so one is steeped in the language and has to learn it: South Africa was a bilingual country and Afrikaans was just a subject, and all lessons in our school were in English. I never did very well in Afrikaans but it was a compulsory subject.

I remember the rules and regulations were very strict at the school. Order marks were dished out left right and centre for things like not wearing the correct shoes, or for wearing a cardigan when out in the street. The only way to dress was either shirtsleeves or with a blazer, and always with a hat. If it was raining we had to wear green berets to protect our hats and leave them at school, so one always had to remember to take the beret in the school satchel. We also had to wear House buttons which were different colours depending which house you belonged to. I was in Kitchener, which was purple, and on the odd occasion that I forgot my House button, someone would have a spare and I would borrow it, but woe betide me if anyone recognized I was wearing the wrong coloured house button.

On Sundays we wore white dresses, all identical, with white gloves and seamed stockings with our brown lace-up school shoes, and our panama hats or berets if it was raining. Before going to church we were lined up and inspected both front and back to make sure our seams were straight and our stockings had no runs, and also that we had money for the collection. Many times if someone didn't have money they would slip their house button into their glove and show the round button stuck in the finger, and vow that it was a coin. This didn't always work!

Mo and Bert took Sue Phillips and me to Durban one Sunday, soon after term began. What a treat we had. We rode in Dodgem boats and were taken for a rickshaw ride; we tasted candy floss for the first time and swam in the ocean. Driving home they took us through the Valley of a Thousand Hills. We had the most spectacular views of a thousand hills wherever you looked.

My mother and brother arrived from Kenya about three months after me having sold up and sorted out our affairs in Kenya, and she rented a house in Winterskloof, outside of Pietermaritzburg. She bought two horses for us to ride and worked as the Headmaster's secretary at the Boys College, which my brother eventually attended.

Life was very hard for my mother. We moved to another house in Winterskloof and then eventually she rented a large house in Pietermaritzburg and took in students from Kenya whose parents were still there. She started complaining of tennis elbow and gave up riding, and then went into hospital for a minor operation during the holidays. Then there were operations every holiday: she had one breast removed and then the other. Every term she went back to work and had all her treatments during the holidays. I would not accept that she had anything terminal, although I had a frightful fear of cancer. My grandmother came out to live with us, as my mother said she had such a guilty conscience that she had done nothing for her all her life, while my aunt had looked after her in the UK. Then my uncle, whom I had never met, came to stay from Canada. My mother was in hospital yet again, and my uncle and grandmother arranged for all our boarders to go elsewhere… I was incensed, and went rushing into hospital and told my mother what was happening. She immediately discharged herself, and my uncle had to take me to one side and explain to me that my mother had ten months to live. It was like the bottom of my world had dropped out: I was 14 years old and about to lose my mother, our family was disintegrating, what would happen to my brother and me without parents?

Those last few weeks were very painful. My mother was the most courageous woman I have ever known. She carried on working at the college, and that last Christmas in 1965 she took a job working in a beautiful hotel in Cape Province, in the middle of nowhere, on the coast at the mouth of the Umgazi River. It was idyllic for us youngsters but my mother became seriously ill, and she took me with her to drive to the nearest town to see a doctor and get morphine, of which she was in dire need. She was so ill, she asked me to drive (I was 15 and not the best person behind a wheel). The hotel was so full that my mother, brother and I had to share a bedroom, which was particularly heartbreaking as my mother was crying out in pain. Eventually, I had to ring my sister and brother-in-law, who were on holiday, and ask them to come and collect us, as my mother was not fit enough to drive all the way back to Natal. She was admitted to hospital on our return where she died six days later, on the 19th of January, 1966.

***

My brother and I were both sent to boarding school after my mother died, and we spent our holidays with Mo and Bert. It wasn't easy for them, as they had just adopted three children, but they became our legal guardians.

I think I was about ten or eleven years old when my mother announced that my half-sister Mo was getting married and that I was to be her bridesmaid. I was very excited, as I had been a bridesmaid with Bella once before, at the wedding of a mutual family friend; Bella had since been a bridesmaid to her brother Pip and would probably be for all her other brothers (there were five in all). Then I heard the news that Mo had called off the wedding and had run off to South Africa with an Afrikaaner—I was so disappointed.

Mo and Bert were the kindest most loving couple I knew. When I first arrived in South Africa, they welcomed me with such warmth, and I was so happy that she married him. It was the right decision. I had never met the person she had left at the altar, but I knew this was right for her.

Every Friday they collected a small boy, Jan, from a children's home to spend the weekend with them. Jan, who was four years old, was paralyzed and wore calipers so he could walk. He was so much fun and simply adored Mo and Bert and referred to them as Mum and Dad. Mo and Bert had been taking Jan out and had him to stay for holidays since he was very small. They had been trying to adopt him for a while—they longed to have a child of their own—but his family would not agree to the adoption. It was so sad.

Before my mother and Andrew arrived from Kenya, Mo and Bert adopted two tow-haired brothers, Andrew and Marcus, three and four years old respectively. Mo and Bert were ideal parents, very

1965 Anna, Peggy and Andrew

1965 Andrew Peggy (in hospital) and Anna with her
favourite dog Taiking

1965 Peggy and Taiking, Andrew and Anna

Marcus, Debbie and Andrew 1966

Candice, Barbara,
"Little Andrew" and Diane, 2005

Bert and Mo

patient and loving: the boys took some time to settle in but when they realised they were there to stay, with a new home and a new Mum and Dad, they were like any other family. I always remember when they met my mother they used to call her 'Piggy' instead of Peggy, and although they had South African accents it was a delight to hear them say 'nooo' and other Scottish pronunciations that they picked up from Mo, whose accent had survived from her childhood in Scotland.

Once Andrew and my mother arrived in South Africa, Andrew was sent to the local prep school in Pietermaritzburg: he had a good friend there, Derek, who had four brothers, and Andrew spent quite a bit of time with their family and Derek came to our house. Andrew came home one day to say that Derek's family was adopting a little girl, Debbie. She was much younger than the boys in the family, and according to Andrew she spent most of her time with an ayah, and was rather neglected by the family. Sometime later Mo and Bert announced they were adopting a little girl, Debbie, and when Andrew met her, he was surprised to find that it was the same Debbie his friend Derek's family had intended to adopt: we were all so happy she joined Mo and Bert's family, as it seemed she was very unhappy with her previous situation. The three children were a delight and it wasn't long before they were one big happy family.

We had very good friends in Kenya who also came to South Africa, the Hartland-Mahons. Their son Marcus had always been good friends with Andrew and they went to the same prep school in Kenya. The family was also very involved with the pony club in Kenya, and both Marcus and Sally, his younger sister, were good riders. Sally was at school with me, but she was several years younger. In South Africa, my mother renewed her friendship with Margaret Hartland-Mahon, who was a godsend to my mother while she underwent surgeries during the holidays: we spent most of our holidays with them on their farm.

Marcus spent time with us when my mother was fit enough, and sometimes we would all be with Mo and Bert: Mo began referring to her children, my brother and his friend as "Big Andrew," "Little

Andrew," "Big Marcus" and "Little Marcus." To this day
she still refers to my brother as "Big Andrew" and her Andrew as
"Little Andrew."

One of the girls boarding with us was Sue Phillips, whose parents ran the Dairy in Molo. She attended Molo school with me, and then we found ourselves at the same school in South Africa. Her parents did not come to South Africa for several years, so she stayed with us during the term and returned to Kenya in the holidays. Her parents eventually moved to South Africa, but they settled in the Transvaal so she continued her schooling in Natal.

Several months after my mother died, I had acute appendicitis and had to be driven to Pietermaritzburg to have my appendix removed. While I was there, Sue came to visit her latest boyfriend who was also there, having had an epileptic fit. She came to visit me and introduced me to her boyfriend. As we were both in the same hospital, he came to visit me and we became very friendly. When I came out of hospital and returned to school he wrote to me and we kept in touch until the holidays, when we started going out together. His name was John and he was the spitting image of one of the Monkeys (the group). We had a very sweet innocent relationship; I was 15 and he was 17. When I told him I was going to England he was very sad and asked if he could drive me to Durban to catch my plane.

Mo and Bert agreed, and we left for the airport on a very hot day in December. I was carrying a sweater with me, as it would be winter when I arrived in England—I had never owned a coat. The worst thing that could have happened did: John's car broke down ten miles from Pietermaritzburg, and we knew Mo and Bert were ahead of us. The only thing we could do was to hitchhike to Durban. There we were on the side of the road hitching a lift to catch my plane. Sweat was pouring from my face, the heat was unbearable, and now I was so worried that we would miss the plane. Thankfully someone stopped and gave us a lift to Durban, and when they heard my tale, they took us straight to the airport. Mo and Bert were furious and said I should have come with them in the first place and I felt duly chastised. Eventually it was time to say goodbye to everyone, Andrew, John, Mo, Bert, and their three children, Andrew, Marcus and Debbie. It was very sad and tearful. I did not know when I would be coming back. I told everyone I would go to England for two years and then I would be back. My brother Andrew and I were not to see each other again for ten years, and it was nearly 40 years before I went back to South Africa, after Bert died and I went over to comfort Mo.

During my 2006 trip to South Africa, to visit Mo after Bert died, I had a three-hour stopover in Johannesburg and Mo had arranged for "Little Andrew" to meet me there with his wife and daughters. What a delight that was! There was this gorgeous 47-year-old hunk with his wife and two daughters, all very attractive and suntanned; his elder daughter was in her final year at university, reading Law, and the younger daughter was about to start her first year. "Little Andrew" was still as fair-haired as I remembered him when he was seven years old, waving goodbye to me at Durban airport when I left for England.

I found out quite recently that my mother was originally planning on going to England after Kenya's Independence, but she had been diagnosed with cancer and Mo had arranged for her to get free treatment in Pietermaritzburg if she was prepared to be a guinea pig for cancer treatment. My mother obviously thought she had nothing to lose, as it seemed the illness was quite advanced: she never let us know she was ill, and even when she had her first and second mastectomies, she carried on as if she had the rest of her life to live.

I also realize that in Kenya, we were probably as poor as church mice, but I never felt it; we never seemed to want for anything. My aunt Lois, who was kept on a very tight budget by her husband in England, held monthly sales to raise money for her church and worthy causes. People would bring in clothes, bikes, furniture, anything that could be sold, and she would keep 10 percent for the church and worthy causes and the owner of the items would collect their money, rather like consignment in the USA. We were obviously one of her worthy causes, and the church had new choir robes, and beautiful hand embroidered hassocks for every seat in the church, with money raised from Lois' sales. Lois bought all the canvasses and wools and gave them to parishioners with coloured wools to make into hassocks using the theme of the Cross, with the main colour being turquoise. Once they did the tapestry, they returned them to Lois who covered leather hassocks with them for the church. This was a ten year project. All those wonderful boxes of clothes she sent us from England were all second-hand, but I had never realised: to me they were wonderful new clothes. I know, having lived with Lois, that she carried on this charitable cause until she stopped doing the sales in her 70s. She particularly helped families from Kenya, as she was the Chairwoman for the East African Women's League for many years.

CHAPTER 3

ENGLAND

Because of apartheid in South Africa no African country would let South African planes fly through their airspace, so I left Durban for Johannesburg and changed planes to fly to England. We flew up the West Coast with two stopovers on islands, off the West coast of Africa.

On arriving at Heathrow I was surprised to find it hard to understand what people were saying. It was like they were speaking a different language. Having lived in South Africa for four years, I realized that I had picked up a strong South African accent and I found the English accent quite foreign now. As I went through Customs, my passport was stamped and in a bewildered state I was trying to find out where I had to go next. Then I heard my name and flight number called over the tannoy, instructing me to go to a certain place, but when I got there found that there were two Anna Murrays on the same flight, and I certainly didn't understand the instructions that were left. As I was wandering around, the Customs man came up to me and asked me where my father was born: when I said in Scotland, and he asked for my passport again and scrubbed out something in it. Later I saw he had originally stamped that I was allowed into the country for three months, but when he found out my father was born in Scotland he deleted that.

Eventually I found the Exit and came out into a sea of faces. I was trying to remember what my aunt Lois looked like: I had met her when she came out to Kenya when I was about nine years old, but I hadn't seen her in seven years. Suddenly there she was, settling a coat around my shoulders and telling me to put it on. What a relief to see her familiar face and know she was in control—it had been very nerve-racking, dealing with Customs and then finding a strange message for me.

It was a cold day and I was disappointed there was no snow; a slight drizzle kept the wipers going intermittently as we drove along the motorway and then turned off towards Maidenhead. We travelled along the River Thames until we reached Cookham village. I tried to remember Cookham: after my father died my mother took leave and brought us to England for a month, we were seven and eight years old and spent a lot of that time in Cookham. As we drove up the single street, I did remember The Old Apothecary (the chemist's shop) and post office on the right, and there was the famous Bel and Dragon which my uncle frequented. It was a very quaint old village and it didn't seem that much had changed. Moor Cottage was almost the last building on the right, a large white house with a fabulous magnolia tree in the front. It was known to be the tallest house in Cookham, and immediately next to it were some small terraced cottages and the last building, almost on the moor was the Crown, our closest pub. I always wondered how such a large house could be called a cottage.

My aunt drove up the drive and around the back to the garages. We unloaded my bags and she took me upstairs to show me my room. What struck me first was how cold it was in the house: when we went upstairs, it seemed to be a few degrees colder. I shivered and asked if there was any heating.

"Yes, we have storage radiators that are charged at night when the power is cheaper and they hold the heat for the day. There is an electric fire in the sitting room, but I only like that used when we are in the room, and I like it switched off when the temperature reaches 60 degrees. In the winter it is necessary to wear lots of layers of sweaters to keep warm."

I was 16 years old and there were two things I simply could not comprehend. One was snow—how did it feel? What was the texture? The second was television: how could they get a picture coming out of a box? I understood a projector and watching a film on a screen, we had one of those at the Highlands Hotel and showed many wonderful black and white movies every Saturday night, but television was something else. I knew I was going to have to wait for snow but I could see the television. I asked Lois if I could watch it; she replied,

"There will be nothing on at this time, it doesn't start until around 5 p.m." So now I had to wait in anticipation. I went back upstairs and unpacked my things, exploring my room at the same time. I found a cupboard door which I opened to find a basin with a large mirror and light overhead. "Well this is a nice idea," I thought. There were two chests of drawers and a built-in wardrobe, and by the window a dressing table and chair. It all looked very comfortable: I only wished it was a little warmer.

My aunt called up to me,

"I am going to take Jemima out for a walk, would you like to come?"

"Yes please, I would love to," as I ran down the stairs to join her.

Jemima was a young boxer and was put on her lead. Lois lent me some wellingtons and we walked down the drive and turned right past the two little cottages and then right down the lane past the Crown. Trying to avoid the puddles, we chatted until we reached the end of the lane where there was a gate and a stile. I had never seen one before. We climbed over the stile and Jemima scrambled through it into a field where Lois let her off the lead. She tore off in great excitement and then came back to us, leaping up to try and grab the lead out of Lois' hand. We arrived at the edge of the Thames. What a beautiful sight. I had never seen such a wide river before, and there were fabulous properties on the other side. One had a boathouse and beautifully manicured lawns leading down to the waters' edge. The one next to that had a profusion of flowers shaped in exquisite flower beds and a pretty gazebo near the river bank. On our side it seemed to be farmland and Lois told me that everyone took their dogs for walks along the river.

On our return to the house, Lois said the television would probably be on, so I rushed into the sitting room and started twiddling knobs. I couldn't find any channels, I had no idea how many I might find, and complained to Lois that I couldn't make it work. I was even worried I had broken it, in my enthusiasm to watch television for the first time. Lois then showed me how and I found there were only two channels anyway, mostly children's programming at that time.

We found I was too young to start training in Hotel Management and Catering, so my aunt sent me to a private secretarial college, which I hated and I vowed at the time I would never work in an office, but in later life was thankful that I had this training. While I was attending the college, I found the local hairdressers' were looking for Saturday help to shampoo. I really enjoyed earning my own pocket money, and they even employed me through the holidays.

When I first arrived in England, Lois introduced me to youngsters of my own age and I met many of my cousin James's (Jamie's) friends, Lois accepted invitations for me to go to teenage parties and arranged a few of my own, but I found it difficult to shake the feeling of being the outsider. I didn't speak like them and had had such a different upbringing—we couldn't seem to find a common ground. My fellow teenagers criticized me for the way I spoke, and I think because no one took any notice of the way I spoke in the hairdressers, I was drawn to the people who worked there—but then I was criticized for spending too much time with the "wrong sort of people." I couldn't seem to win, and felt I wasn't good enough for Lois's friends. I felt particularly left out when during the summer holidays Lois and Jamie went on holiday to Sark in the Channel Islands and I was left at home with my uncle, who was a very grumpy old man and spent his whole life in his little room in the front of the house.

Memories came back to me about something my mother once said to me when I was a child at the Highlands Hotel. Every Sunday Andrew and I were allowed a Sunday soda, whatever brand or flavor we liked; the rest of the week we were restricted to water or orange squash (orange squash, for those who don't know it, is a revoltingly sweet orange-flavoured cordial diluted with water).

Once when I asked my mother if I could have a soda on another day, she said, "When you can pay for your own, you can have as many sodas as you wish, but I am only paying for you to have one a week." I never asked again, and I suppose I thought of this when Lois and Jamie went on holiday and left me at home. I thought when I can afford to go on holiday I will, but I would not expect someone else to pay for it. I have never expected anyone to pay for my pleasures, but I have been blessed on many occasions and have always been very thankful and appreciative, but I would never take anyone's generosity for granted.

In September, just before my seventeenth birthday, I was accepted at the Redesdale Arms in Gloucestershire. Moreton-in-Marsh was a charming Gloucestershire village, built in traditional Cotswold stone. The Redesdale Arms was a training hotel for "educated young ladies," and although I thought the regime very strict, I think it taught me values and to strive for perfection.

At 7 a.m. we were expected in the kitchen in our blue overalls, to take early morning tea trays to guests. The trays had to be laid a certain way and had been checked the night before. Those girls not on tea tray duty cleaned the dining room and bar. There was a particular way to do this, and woe betide anyone that skimped on it. Once the dining room was cleaned and polished, breakfast was laid on the table, with grapefruit, mangoes, pineapple and various cereals, milk and sugar. Two girls stayed to serve breakfast, taking orders for bacon and eggs, kippers or omelets if wanted, and everyone was served with toast, marmalade and tea or coffee.

Every girl had three bedrooms to clean and one person had all the bathrooms to do. As soon as guests started coming down to breakfast we would go and do our rooms. Again, this was a very thorough job and every room was checked over to make sure there was no dust on picture frames or under beds. Once all the rooms were done we would have lunch and change into starched white overalls to serve the guests' lunch. While lunch was being served the rooms were checked and if they were not done correctly, we would be called aside and told to go and redo whichever room was not perfect. It was heartbreaking: one would find the room with everything pulled out and left in a pile in the middle. If the bed was not correctly made it was pulled apart. It certainly made you take care of doing things correctly.

During lunch one person was allocated to cleaning the silver-ware. All the cutlery and jugs and sugar basin were silver and had to be cleaned correctly. With constant use and going through the dishwasher they got tarnished very quickly.

The attention to detail was drummed into us, not through words but by having to redo anything that was not up to the expected standard. The lessons I learnt at the Redesdale Arms have stayed with me all my life: to this day I am a perfectionist.

Although this was my chosen profession, life was not easy for me. The English way of life was very different from my African upbringing: I was not used to seasons, I hated wearing a coat in the winter, and I felt very restricted after the freedom of Africa. I had a ghastly South African accent that everyone seemed to make fun of, and I was extremely naïve as far as girls and boys were concerned. I seemed to be forever teased, and felt that I was never going to become an "educated young lady."

The following year I continued my training at the Parkhill Hotel in Lyndhurst, and I chose to specialize in cooking. I had a very good friend here who had also just lost her mother and we felt like kindred spirits: Frances and I often travelled up to Cookham to stay with my aunt, or we would go to the West Country and stay with Frances's family. In those days everyone hitch-hiked everywhere if they didn't have transport, and that is how we got around. On one of our journeys up to Cookham we got a lift in a jaguar, a very old car with leather seats and beautiful polished wood dashboard. The driver was a young man of 24, Ted and his friend Tom, who was older. With quite a long drive we chatted and found they lived in Southampton, and exchanged names and addresses. A few days later Ted telephoned Frances and asked her out, and he also had a friend and asked if I would join them. I didn't like his friend and so didn't see him again, but Frances continued to date Ted for a while, until she decided to leave the Parkhill and go and work at a Western riding school. Ted then invited me out and we started a serious relationship.

I introduced Ted to my aunt, but she took an immediate dislike to him—she told me he wasn't from our "class." I was having a lot of problems with this concept of social classes: I knew what life was like under apartheid, but where I had grown up, purely social distinctions had never been recognized. I eventually went to live with Ted, which sent my aunt into turmoil. She had a private investigator check him out and told me he was a womanizer and already had a child by another unmarried girl, and told me I *must* leave him. That was the key word: *must*. I was already smitten with Ted, and then found I was pregnant. This was a completely different ball game.

I had no idea what was I going to do, who was I going to turn to… Ted decided to take me away to the Norfolk Broads where we hired a boat and had a blissful few days, until we returned the boat. Police were waiting for us, and arrested Ted. It seemed he had been paying for everything by writing cheques, which then bounced, and the boat hire people called the police. He was charged and let out on bail, and we returned home to work out how he could pay it all back. He couldn't see how to do it and suggested we go on the run, as now we had the police after him and my aunt after me; I often wonder why I even considered it, but on reflection I realise how desperately insecure I was. I had no parents, and now I was going to have a child that I really wanted more than anything else. It would give me the family I so longed for, and I really didn't feel I could hope for any help from my aunt as I had already disobeyed her.

We packed very few things and bought train tickets to Cork, Ireland, including the ferry. On the train we decided on new names Jane and Steve, and Ted insisted I tear up my passport and any other documents with my old name on it. This whole escape seemed so exciting to me, although I knew it was all wrong. In my young eyes I couldn't see any alternative but to follow Ted and hope he would look after me. We found our way to Bantry Bay on the West coast of Ireland: it wasn't long before we found a small cottage to rent, and Ted found a job working in a shrimp factory. Castletownbearhaven was a charming village on the edge of Bantry Bay. Looking out to sea, we could see the huge oil tankers coming into the bay and I just prayed that nothing would cause them to have a spillage. Ted brought crabs home for me to process for the factory, a very time-consuming and fiddly job, but between us we brought the pennies in, to live on.

Ted was very keen fisherman, so we often took a boat out in the bay: he would give me a line with six hooks on it and let me drop it over the side of the boat. Within minutes I could feel the pull of a catch and often find all six hooks with writhing, silvery-blue mackerel fighting to get away. We would row back to the beach, gather some dry wood and Ted would light a fire. While it was getting to the right temperature Ted cleaned and gutted several mackerel and wrapped them in large leaves and put them on the fire to cook. These were the most delicious fish I had ever tasted. He explained that they stayed blue only while they were really fresh: they turned silvery green after an hour or so.

It wasn't long before Ted got fed up with Ireland and decided we should head back to England. I was pretty desperate too: we had no home for our child and had bought nothing for its arrival, and I could see no future at all. We arrived at Dublin airport and Ted handed himself into the police. They flew us back to the UK and Ted was taken straight to Wandsworth prison and charged with fraud. I had to eat humble pie and ring my aunt and tell her the situation: she, of course, came and collected me and brought me home to Cookham.

Anthony was born on Friday the 13th of February, while Ted was in prison and my aunt happened to be away. I was alone in the house and called an ambulance at 2 a.m. I spent the rest of the night and next day in labour, with no one even knowing I was giving birth. I had left a note on the dresser in the hall: when my aunt arrived back on the 14th, she came to see me in hospital, and said that no way was this baby coming home to her house—his birth on Friday the 13th was a very bad omen. She spent many hours trying to persuade me that he must be adopted, asking what future could I give him as a single mother? I have never felt so bad, inferior and helpless. I had no one on my side except this gorgeous little bundle who I clung to desper-ately: I was really at the mercy of others, as I had no home to take him to and no means of earning a living in the immediate future.

CHAPTER 4

ANTHONY

It was 1985, and for the first time in my life I felt that life, at last, was wonderful. Anthony was 15 and doing well at his public school: he excelled in Sports and had even played in the 1st XI cricket team, younger than all his 18-year-old his team mates. I was so proud of him… He had said he wanted to play cricket for England, but even he realized it is only the very top elite players that get to do that, so his plan b was to serve his country in the Army. His ambition was to go to Sandhurst and with school guidance had been recommended to join the Royal Engineers in Intelligence. His future was so sure.

Looking back over the years, I could hardly believe we had got so far. I had a wonderful job working for Sir Neville and Lady Bowman Shaw and their four children: the youngest, Justin, was nearly the same age as Anthony. We lived in a beautiful apartment on Toddington Manor Estate, which boasted a private cricket pitch, swimming pool, tennis court and squash court, all the sports that Anthony excelled in. It was truly heavenly for both of us.

This was a long way from how it all started 15 years before. I had won the battle with my aunt, and Anthony came back with me to her house from the hospital. Within a few weeks I got myself a job working for IBM whose offices were just across the moor from the house and my aunt looked after Anthony for the few hours I worked. When Anthony was six months old I found a job as a housekeeper to a divorced man and his daughter near Eastbourne. My aunt kindly drove me down to my new job, but within days I realized that this man was really looking for a lover/wife; I was 19 and certainly not looking for a lover/husband, not when it was being forced upon me. Again my aunt came to the rescue and brought me back to Cookham.

A friend I had met in Cookham, Carol, who had married Tony Best when I first arrived in the UK, lived in Crowborough, Sussex, and introduced me to a family, Shirley and Breon Rawlings, who were looking for a housekeeper/childminder and offered separate

Anthony and Pippa aged 2 years old

Anthony and Pippa with Vron, Clapham Common

Anna and Anthony 1980

Anthony at a cricket match 1981

accommodation with a garden and full use of a car. This was ideal: it gave me some independence from my aunt and I could work in the house while Anthony was sleeping. My apartment was adjoining, so I could leave the doors open even when he was awake, and he would play for hours in his playpen.

Then Ted was released from prison and came looking for me. He persuaded me to marry him: we got married at the Registry Office in Crowborough with the cleaner as a witness. He very soon got tired of living in "my" house and decided we had to move on, so we moved to Sissinghurst, a tiny village not far from Cranbrook. The house was tiny, damp and not suitable for a young family with a baby. He seemed to have found a reasonable job which supplied him with a car, but he did have to work late, and often came home to change to go out on "business" in the evenings. Ted was not interested in Anthony and hated it when the baby cried. I tried to make sure he was asleep by the time Ted came home, so as not to cause him to get angry. One night with deep snow outside he came home and demanded his supper, showered and got ready to spend an evening watching TV. The baby was grizzling in his cot, which infuriated him, and he went in there and beat the living daylights out of Anthony. When I tried to stop him, he grabbed me and bodily threw me out, with very little clothing on, into the snow, and locked the door. Thank goodness Anthony had learnt how to climb out of his cot: I went to the window outside, which was fortunately rotten, inched it open and gesticulated to Anthony to come to me. The house was so small, our dining room table was stored in Anthony's bedroom, and on it were two large bath sheets. He climbed out of his cot and clambered on the table, with the help of a chair, and I whispered to pass me the towels, and I grabbed him out of the window and ran with both of us wrapped in towels. We went to the car, but Ted had taken the keys, and we were too far from anywhere to try and walk, so we spent the night in the car.

This was only one of many such experiences we had to endure. The November I turned 21, Ted took me shopping and bought me a twin-tub washing machine (this was going to be the first time I didn't have to hand wash all Anthony's nappies and clothes, it was a dream come true), then on my birthday he wasn't there, and then I received a message to say he had left me… a week later, the store where he bought the washing machine called round for the first payment. Well I had nothing, no money and no husband, so they took it away, with my dream…

Like a bad penny, Ted returned, and as always I was ready to forgive him. He was very apologetic and suggested that we have a big party for the New Year. I loved to entertain, but somehow I couldn't put my heart into this party. He had let me down so badly and I had lost faith in him. Was he going to leave me again? I was still so raw from him leaving me in November. I knew I had to go along with him, if I was going to give our marriage any chance.

I should have seen the warning signs, especially when Ted never once suggested I invite any of my friends. This was definitely his party, and I did not know many of the people invited. Ted had another life which did not include me and I was going to meet them tonight.

Ted went shopping and I cooked special dishes for the party and cleaned our tiny house. I arranged a table with a cloth on it for the drinks and put all the glasses out, and near the kitchen I had another table, where I arranged flowers in the centre, to be used for the food.

As I watched the guests arrive, I realised that most of them were girls, alone or in pairs. One girl promptly left when she found out he was married; others got really wound up and angry. The whole evening was a farce. I decided then and there that I would take the first opportunity to get out, get away from him for good: I had no money, no work, and didn't know where to go with my nearly two-year-old child, but I had to leave.

Again my aunt came to the rescue, and told me that Vron Addington, the daughter of a great friend of hers, had a two year old daughter and an apartment in London, and was looking for someone in similar circumstances to share. My old friend Alex from my Redesdale days came and collected us and took us to our new home in Princes Gate Mews, an extremely smart address in London.

Vron and her daughter Pippa became life-long friends, and over the years we have kept in touch. Pippa married a Frenchman and now has two children of her own; they live in France. It brings a big ache to my heart, when I think of those two lovely children, Pippa and Anthony aged two, sliding down a bank of autumn leaves…

In London, I did what I had once sworn I would never do: I found a job as a secretary, and was thankful that I had the qualifications for it. I found a good day care centre for Anthony in Chelsea, and my new life without Ted began.

When my mother died, all her worldly belongings, family silver, furniture etc., was sold and a small inheritance was left for Andrew and me when we reached the age of 21: about six months before by 21st birthday the lawyers in South Africa contacted me and asked me where I wanted the money sent. At that time I was married to Ted, and as he had had problems opening a bank account after his little contretemps with cheques, I had suggested we hold a joint account: that was the biggest mistake of my life! While we were still living with the Rawlings, he had grand ideas about buying a boat and sailing to South Africa, so he borrowed money on our joint account and bought a gaff cutter sailing boat. This proved a disaster—he capsized it near Portsmouth and had to be rescued by the Navy. He then decided to sell it, but it was now damaged and of course did not get the price he originally paid. All was fine until I tried to retrieve the money my mother had left me: the bank said they would not release it until the loan was paid off. I am sure to this day Ted never paid off the loan and I never received a penny of my mother's legacy.

Vron was a wonderful influence on me and introduced me to the summer Proms at the Albert Hall. She arranged exclusive little supper parties for some close friends at the mews (mews are restored stables and carriage houses in little cobbled alleys), and afterwards we would walk up to the Albert Hall for a concert where sometimes we were fortunate to have a wonderful orchestra and a famous conductor. I so enjoyed these evenings that for years I arranged with friends to have a night out at the Proms.

Vron arranged one lovely supper party where I met a young lieutenant who was based at Buckingham Palace. A few days later I received a telephone call from him asking me to lunch that day: I accepted and asked where we were to meet, and he told me St James' Palace at noon. Fortunately my office was not too far away; I arrived on time, imagining that we would go to a cosy café somewhere close. Imagine my surprise when I announced myself at the door and was ushered into a large drawing-room, full of the high society of London. My young lieutenant, James, came up and greeted me and I was introduced to Lord such and such and Lady so and so, as a butler came round offering drinks. I was completely over-awed and felt severely underdressed, as I had come straight from the office—and I certainly never drank during the day while working. I took the drink and sipped it very slowly. Once all the guests had arrived, the butler announced "Luncheon is served."

We were shown into an enormous dining room with a huge table seating twenty people and a sparkling chandelier above. The table was laid with masses of beautiful silver, and I hoped that I could figure out which were the correct knives and forks for which dish. There were four crystal glasses at the right hand side of each place setting, and my immediate thought was 'more drinks?' Down the centre of the table was a lovely flower arrangement with silver pheasants on either side, and two large candelabras at each end of the table.

Soup was brought out first, served with a nice white wine: that was easy, I knew which was the soup spoon. The wine glass and soup plates were cleared away and next we had a sole bonne femme; I glanced over at James and followed suit as he picked up the outer knife and fork. The next glass was filled with more white wine. Once the glasses and plates had been cleared a second time, dinner plates were placed in front of us and a waiter came round with a large silver salver and served us thinly sliced roast lamb with roast potatoes, caramelised carrots, Brussels sprouts and parsnips, followed by another waiter with gravy, mint sauce and red currant jelly on his salver. Red wine was served with the lamb.

I sipped the different wines, and quite quickly began to feel quite heady and carefree, even though I still had to get back to the office and do some work. Lemon meringue pie was offered for dessert, with a sweet white wine. This was followed by cheese and biscuits and more red wine. Coffee and liqueurs followed. How anyone could work after that feast, I have no idea. I duly said my goodbyes and thanked James for inviting me, and left for my office. I have never felt so light-headed and incapable of work, but it was an experience I would never forget. I certainly had a lot to tell my friends back at work when I returned two hours late!

Anthony was of course the centre of my life. The terrible twos is definitely a true saying, and strangely enough it seems to affect boys more than girls, I think. One morning I woke up to find my contact lens case empty and broken pieces of plastic lying on the carpet: Anthony had come into my room while I was still asleep, and took them out, chewed them and spat them onto the floor. In those days contact lenses cost me nearly a month's salary. Wall plugs had to be checked to see how they worked; vases had to be examined (and broken); riding the "milko" (a seat on child's milk truck) around the coffee table at full speed was a favourite pastime, knocking mugs or ornaments off the table. Pippa was always far more genteel—Anthony was a tiny daredevil.

I remember one year when he was about five years old, coming downstairs to find all the presents around the tree unwrapped. The few presents that were worthless to a five year old had been left lying around amongst the debris of wrapping paper; all others were gone! I eventually found most of the presents hidden in his room, but I never managed to find out exactly who had given a few of them.

It was hard work, raising my small boisterous son while holding down a full time job during the day and working in a pub in the evenings. One day, Breon Rawlings rang me out of the blue and asked if I would consider returning to them, working as his secretary rather than the housekeeper. I jumped at this opportunity, as I had been very happy working for them in the past; London was not the place of my choice—I'm a real country girl at heart. I returned to Crowborough and my old flat and managed to get Anthony into Dr Bernado's Day Care Centre, which was open all year round. Life was looking up. I stayed with them for three years until Anthony was old enough to go to school.

I had heard that Holmewood House School in Langton Green, the prep school James Rawlings had been attending, was looking for matrons; I thought that would be an ideal job for me, so I could get the holidays off to be with Anthony. I rang up and went for the interview only to be told they didn't need any more matrons. They were, however, looking for a caterer. I told them I had trained in Catering and Hotel Management—they offered me the job on the spot.

Anthony attended the local primary school, as he was not yet old enough to go to Holmewood House, and we were given a very nice school house to live in. I also met a very nice man of whom I became very fond, Norman Nichols. Anthony adored him and he seemed fond of us both, but having just gotten divorced he was in no hurry to rush back into marriage. Norman was to have a profound effect on me for most of my life.

Bad luck struck again: while working in the kitchen I injured my back and was taken to hospital and put in traction for four weeks. My aunt, who had just had a cataract operation on her eyes, came down to Kent and suggested she take Anthony home with her until I was back on my feet. This was a relief for me, as various teachers at Holmewood had been looking after him. During this time Norman met someone else, Aileen, whom he eventually married. I was heartbroken, and concentrated on trying to get myself back on my feet and fit for work, but the orthopaedic surgeon had told me I would not be able to go back to such a physically strenuous job. I found another job with lighter duties, but the accommodation was just one bedroom. I took the position while looking for something more suitable for Anthony and me.

Anthony was six years old, and had been with my aunt for a few months when she rang me up to tell me I would have to have Anthony adopted, as she was going to visit her daughter Penny in America. My hands were tied: I had nowhere for us to live together and this ultimatum from my aunt. I agreed to have him fostered "with a view to adoption" in order to buy time to find a proper place to live. I met the family, who lived in North London (with the accent to prove it), but decided beggars can't be choosers, and agreed to let them foster my Anthony. They had two daughters, and had lost a son to leukemia. I visited Anthony every other weekend.

In the meantime, I had met up with an old buddy of Norman's, Brian Black, whose long-term live-in girl friend had just left him for someone else. He courted me, took me to lovely places for dinner and even came to visit Anthony with me. He then asked me to move in with him, and I thought this might be the answer to all my problems. My only problem was that I wasn't in love with him: I was still trying to get over Norman.

Finally I accepted his offer and moved in; I then asked if he would mind if Anthony came and lived with us. I was shocked by his immediate, adamant refusal; no way would he allow Anthony to come and live with us. He had three children of his own and only had them for visits once a month. He also tried to persuade me to let Anthony be adopted, as I had nothing I could offer him. I was taking a secretarial refresher course in Eastbourne, and being pressured by Brian, my aunt, and Anthony's foster family, all of whom tried to convince me that I was being totally selfish if I didn't let him go. I felt like a cornered fox with no one to turn to.

Looking back, I suppose I really had been brainwashed and made to feel utterly inadequate: everyone had convinced me that Anthony had a far better chance of a good life with this family than he would with me. Brian decided to take a cruise in the Caribbean, and while he was away I had time to think on my own. Finally I rang the family and said they could go ahead with the adoption. It was the worst day of my life. The day before Brian was due home, I had a phone call from the family to say they could not adopt Anthony after all, as he was so strange: he kept wetting his bed, telling them that I didn't love him, he was afraid in the playground and was hiding in corners, and that I must be dead. The next day I drove to North London and collected him. For one week we lived in Brian's car, because I had nowhere else to go. By this time my sweet little boy was speaking with a strong north London accent, but at least we were together. Still, we had nowhere to go and no roof over our heads. In desperation I went to the local Social Services. They helped me find a local foster family on a farm, and I rented a room not far from my college course. Brian had the decency to allow me to keep the car until I was more settled, but I realized that he was definitely not for me. Anthony came to stay with me in my room every weekend, and we took one step at a time.

In 1977, Jubilee Year, and Anthony and I went back to Langton Green to watch the cricket. Norman was the Captain of the team, and they were having a special Jubilee match. While waiting for tea, I saw an old face from the past, John Richards, who with his wife, Sunny, were great friends of the Rawlings; he was walking by with his son Christopher. The last time I had seen them, Sunny was in hospital being treated for cancer, so I stopped and asked how she was and he almost broke down to say she had died six months earlier. I was so saddened, as she was only 35 and such a nice person, leaving a 12-year-old son and 14-year-old daughter. We chatted and John invited Anthony and me over the following weekend for lunch and swimming.

It was a hot summer's day when I collected Anthony from the foster family. We had our bathing costumes packed in the car, and on our way to John's house we stopped off at the garden centre, where I bought some flowers for John's mother. It was a fun lunch with the children bombing each other in the pool and races to see who was the fastest. John asked me if I would like to move into their house and help him with the children and his ageing mother, who lived in the granny flat above the garage. I asked about Anthony coming too, and John said not immediately, but certainly during the holidays, when my course had finished and I could be home with them all. He was very concerned that his children might feel jealous, and they certainly felt deprived of a mother.

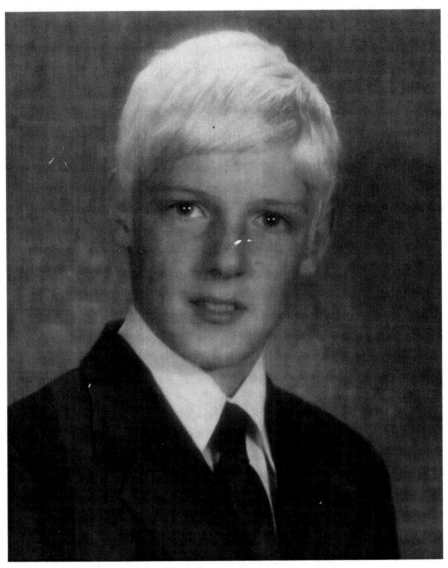

Anthony 1983

I arranged to move in the following weekend. After a pleasant dinner of "poor man's asparagus" (the stems of Swiss chard) and some fresh Dover sole served with the greens of the Swiss chard, I helped John water his fairly large vegetable garden. A visitor came down the garden through the hedge at the back. I was introduced to Brian Hawkins, and we all sat down by the pool with a glass of red wine. Brian and his wife, Judy, lived in the large house behind John's, where they also had a pool and sauna, and Brian extended an invitation for me to come up and swim or use the sauna whenever I liked. I found out that John went up to their house every Sunday night to play snooker, and I was invited as well, where I met Judy and we spent the evening chatting while the men played snooker. A very pleasant evening, but there was just something very special about Brian, and I couldn't put my finger on it.

Once we all settled in and I finished my secretarial course, I started applying for jobs. Again Carol and Tony Best, who had recommended me to the Rawlings many years before, came to the rescue. Tony was looking for a secretary/personal assistant and offered me the job. Tony had inherited his father's business, Rowland Ward, Taxidermists for Big Game Hunters. We were dealing with clients from all over the world who sent their trophies to Rowland Ward to be dressed or processed as heads on walls or elephant feet tables, lion skin rugs, elephant tusks, etc.—many of the animals in the Natural History Museum were processed by Rowland Ward. It was very interesting. Rowland Ward produced a book of World Records every few years, so measurements of different species were taken for the Record Books.

One day a Sheik who had a modeled elephant in his courtyard rang to ask if it could be repaired: that was the day we had an elephant roll into the driveway. It was a full-size bull elephant with large tusks, and had been towed on a low loader. It must have looked quite a sight on the main roads, and it certainly was a talking point in the driveway with the Mill wheel and trace behind it.

Once I was established in my new job, I brought Anthony to John's house at the weekends. One Friday, when I collected him from the foster family, I found he had bruises on his face, and when questioned he told me he had tripped over a toy tractor. I wasn't really sure of this story, as Anthony was as nimble as they come and I couldn't believe he would bruise his face from a fall. So I questioned him several times over the weekend, and he eventually owned up, that the young son of the family he was fostered with had beaten him up. The other boy was 12 years old and Anthony was 7. I reported this to the caseworker, and the following weekend he had more bruises and completely denied being touched by anyone. He vowed he had fallen down the stairs. He was very quiet and didn't want to talk about his activities of the week. I was very worried, and by now I was earning a fairly reasonable salary, so I found a preparatory school not too far away where he could go as a boarder.

In England it isn't easy to just take your child out of foster care once you have voluntarily put him or her there: so I set the stage, and then went and collected him as normal. Anthony looked worse than ever before, and I said nothing to the family but I did not return him on the Sunday night. I rang the caseworker, and told her to come and look at him and said that Anthony would not be going back. I had arranged a private school for him and he would be living with us from now on.

It was sometime later that I found out the truth about what had been going on, and it wasn't from Anthony but from my aunt, nearly a year later. He was staying with her and she had made him some shepherd's pie, which he refused to eat. She tried to coax him and asked him what the matter was, as she knew he loved shepherd's pie. Eventually he broke down and told her it looked like faeces, just like the foster boy had made him eat. In fact, she found out several other awful things that happened to him while he was there. It was nauseating stuff that a 7-year-old could not possibly know. I was devastated to find out what he had been through in the few months he was there. It seemed to go from bad to worse, and I was only thankful that I had been in a position to get him out of it. When he told me he had been beaten up and I reported it to the caseworker, he got into worse trouble with the family, so he never admitted it again. I reported all I had heard to the caseworker, and she said the only way we could pursue it was for Anthony to stand up in court and tell his story. He never ever told me the story, and I was not going to put him through that, so there went another child-molesting family. I couldn't do anything about it.

We lived at John's house for a couple of years. His house was two miles down a very bumpy, unpaved road, and it was very peaceful at the edge of the forest, with only one other house further down the road. All the children got some sort of stability and a routine was set. In the end I decided that Anthony and I needed a place of our own. He had had a few very rough years and it was time to make a home that was ours, not someone else's.

We moved to a village not far away. My job with Tony was coming to an end, as they had banned big game hunting all over the world, and Rowland Ward was folding up. I got a job as a sales manager's secretary, which was very easy, five days a week, 8 a.m. to 4 p.m., leave your work at the office type of job. While there I was head-hunted by another firm who had just invented the automatic light switch and was offered a package I could not refuse, so I travelled a bit further, up to Croydon.

I met a pediatrician named Tony Bennett who practiced in Wimpole Street, in London. He lived in the city during the week, but spent his weekends in Sussex, and his house was not far from mine. I frequently joined him for lunch or dinner and we often popped over the road to his local pub for drinks. We enjoyed each other's company and he joined me at a cricket match at Anthony's school, although he had to be careful, as Anthony was very possessive of his mum. During the holidays we would go over to Tony's for lunch and he and Tony would play darts in the garden. I was getting a bit of a cold response from Anthony: this guy wasn't a physical sportsman, he preferred to watch his sport on the box, and he loved fishing—boring.

During the term time I saw much more of Tony and went up to London and stayed with him there. I spent one week decorating his whole house: as he used to say to me give him a sick child and he could mend it, but he was completely useless in practical terms.

During one of my stays, we woke up early one morning to hear that Britain had declared war on Argentina, and was going to take back the Falkland Islands. Tony said

"Oh Lord, I am a reserve on the medical team." I asked how he had become a reserve, and he told me he was in the Royal Navy most of his life as a doctor, and when he retired he studied to become a pediatrician. I told him he was far too old and not to worry, I was sure they wouldn't call him up. He was 45 years old.

They didn't call him up. Now Tony, in my eyes was a wonderful man, he had served in the Royal Navy all his life; he had "rooms" in Wimpole Street (Harley and Wimpole Streets are where all the specialists and doctors strive to be) as a pediatrician; he was divorced, his children were grown up and married, how lucky could I be? He also seemed to like children—after all, he was a pediatrician.

He told me he was Princess Diana's pediatrician for the child she was about to give birth to. I was amazed and wasn't sure how I could verify this, but why would he not tell me the truth.

Driving between London and Sussex he would say, "Do you see that black BMW two cars behind us? Those are my minders."

"Why would you need minders? I asked.

"Well, I am going to be looking after the future King of England's health." I was speechless, not really knowing whether he was telling me the truth.

I invited Tony up to Cookham to meet my aunt, and she thought he was wonderful. She took us to dinner at the Bel and Dragon, and then she asked him,

"What do you see in this?" She pointed to me like I was a pair of old shoes.

"To tell you the truth, I find Anna very beautiful. She is cheerful and works so hard, we have a lot of laughs together and I love her cooking, and I love her." Wow. My heart swelled and my face turned red—no one had ever complimented me like that before. I had obviously chosen the right one in Lois' eyes, at long last!

Tony then officially proposed to me: he didn't have a ring, but he asked me to marry him. He told me that Prince Charles had given him some Welsh gold that he was having made up into engagement and wedding rings. I was completely bowled over.

A few weeks later Lois invited Tony and me to dinner; she had also invited Vron and her new man, Sam Mainds, whom she was going to marry. Tony and Sam, who was a QC, got on famously: they had the same sense of humour, and it was lovely to see Vron again. Lois put on a sumptuous meal for us and served it at the table on large platters for us to help ourselves, until it came time for the dessert. She had made her usual raspberry whip (pureed raspberries mixed with whipped cream). She proceeded to serve us rather than let us serve ourselves as we had done with the other courses. I asked for a small portion, as I am not fond of desserts.

"You will take what I give you and eat it!" She served me first and brought the plate round to my place. I passed it on to one of the guests, as I thought I was family, and she immediately whipped it away and slammed it down in front of me again.

"Lois, please may I have a smaller portion."

"No, you eat what you are given."

I was so embarrassed by this time, I asked Tony to take me home. Tony made faces and persuaded me to stay. How could she talk to me like this in front of guests?

When the coffee was served, I just took it, although I didn't want it; she plopped cream in it, whether I wanted it or not, and I just left it, so as not to have to say anything else. It was such a lovely evening, and now it was finishing on this sour note. I was used to this type of treatment on our own, but not with company.

Tony made one big mistake with me: he invited one of his ex-naval colleagues, Giles, and his wife, Nora, for the weekend in the country, and I cooked a lovely meal for us all. They were perfectly charming guests and we had a wonderful weekend together. On the Sunday afternoon, the four of us went for a walk in the country and we paired up and chatted along the way. I asked Giles about Tony being the future King's pediatrician (the baby hadn't been born yet).

"What bull!" he said, "He is no more going to be the future King's pediatrician, than I am the Queen Mum." I couldn't believe it; he had even told Lois the same story. I asked Giles not to mention anything as I would deal with it in my own way.

We waved them goodbye, and instead of me staying over, I made excuses to leave, and he said "Perhaps it is a good thing, as I have to go up to London, as I have an early appointment with Princess Diana."

"That will be the last lie you tell me." I announced. "You are not their pediatrician and never will be. Why did you have to tell me such wild stories? In my eyes you were pretty marvelous without those, now you've blown it. Bye."

I was pretty heartbroken at first, but I was glad I found out when I did. We had both been invited to the House of Lords for Vron and Sam's wedding—Vron's father was Viscount Sidmouth, so they were allowed to be married there. I was so looking forward to going to the wedding but having just called everything off with Tony I didn't feel strong enough to go on my own.

Anthony was doing very well at his prep school, and he loved it. He excelled in all sports: he got his Colours for cricket, won all the field events at sports day and also won the Swimming Cup. Then I had a letter from the school to say it was closing down: this was so sad as he really enjoyed it. It had small classes and it really gave him the feeling of belonging. He only had one more year before going up to public school, so I found another private school not too far from us, called Temple Grove; the fees were far too high for me, so I sent him there as a day boy instead of a boarder, but I think he really missed boarding, as on Sundays he would go into school on his bike and join his buddies, playing cricket or swimming or playing football. Temple Grove was a much larger school and the competition far harder, but he still managed to get in all the sports teams and win the Senior Cross Country Cup. He sat his Common Entrance Exam, and we went around the country looking at schools and sitting their exams, and he eventually got into Lord Wandsworth College.

I began to get cold feet as the time drew closer for Anthony to start at public school. I had had him home for one year and had got used to it; I was going to miss him at weekends, so I decided to look for a live-in job as a cook, where I would be working weekends. One job looked particularly interesting, so I rang them and they asked me to come for an interview. I arrived in Toddington and found the driveway down to the manor house. There was a cute little cottage at the entrance to the driveway, and as I drove down I had to stop the car: there was a breathtaking view of farm buildings to my left, and in front of these a full-size cricket pitch led down to a pond with an island of willows. Beyond this sat the lovely pink manor house. I carried on down the driveway and found there was another pond on the other side, with ducks and two black swans, and on the bank leading back up to the cricket pitch were about 50 Canada geese. The fields beyond were all crops that had already been harvested, and some even ploughed ready for the next crop. As far as the eye could see were enormous fields at harvest time. I drove by the house until I came to a large archway leading into to an enchanting courtyard, with the back of the house on my left and what looked like garages and stables (the garages were originally for the carriages). Above the garages were delightful dormered windows with pretty curtains.

I parked the car and Georgina Bowman-Shaw came to greet me, with two little Norwich terriers and a labrador in tow. I was invited inside and shown the kitchen, which was beautiful with a green 4-oven Aga. The kitchen was decorated in blue and yellow, with a large work surface in the middle of the kitchen with cupboards underneath. There was plenty of room to prepare the best fare. Work surfaces were all around the kitchen with cupboards above and below, and next to the big American fridge was a door that led to a larder with mesh on the windows and two pheasants hanging. There was a marble surface all round the larder, somewhere cool to keep food.

After making coffee, we went through to the snug room and the dogs leapt on to their beanbags and Lara the labrador flopped down on to hers. After a pleasant chat and discussing what was required of the job, Lady Bowman Shaw said she would ring me and let me know as soon as possible. She had a few more interviews to see first.

Just two days later Lady Bowman Shaw rang me and offered me the job. I was delighted and I knew Anthony would love his new home. He began his new term at Lord Wandsworth College and a few weeks later I moved all our belongings (including cats) up to Toddington.

Thus began a most idyllic part of our lives. I had a fabulous job, which I loved, and Anthony did very well at school, again getting in to the main teams—football, rugby and cricket. I became a cricket mum, sitting on the sidelines with my knitting. Anthony invited me to most of his matches, if he thought I could make it. His Under-14 team won the Hampshire cup, so the following year they played the nationals against winners of the other counties. They didn't have these matches printed up in their term schedule, as they were played as time allowed, and they were knock-out matches, so if they didn't win the match they were out of the competition. I was invited to all these matches until they were eventually knocked out. I also went to watch regular matches against other schools, and sometimes there might only be two parents as spectators. I mentioned to Anthony that if he didn't want to ask me to come to every match, I would not be offended.

"Oh no, Mum, I play so much better when you are there."

Anthony rang me up one day, very excited. "Can you come to the 1st XI match against the Old Boys? I've been asked to play in the 1st XI."

"Of course I will try and come to that! How exciting to be chosen to play."

I arrived in plenty of time before the match; I parked my car in a good spot by the field, and Anthony and several of his buddies came to join. I had brought the usual cake and several goodies for his team mates—Anthony hated cake but he liked me to bring one anyway, as his friends loved it. Today, there were masses of spectators and cars parked around the perimeter of the field. Next to me, lying on a rug on the grass by their car, were two young men around 21 years old. The game began with Anthony opening the bowling and in the first over (six deliveries) he eliminated three batsmen from the other team.

The two young men got up and went over to the scoreboard while the bowlers were changing, and came back saying, "That boy is only 14 years old!" I was so proud of my son.

When it was their turn to bat, Anthony went in as fourth batsman, and he was still there at the end of the match. The 1st XI won against the Old Boys, who were all out. After the match Anthony came over with his buddies to enjoy the cake, cookies and crisps I had brought, and washed it down with a coke.

Anthony never lost his daredevil character. One day I received a telephone call from his housemaster to say that Anthony had been "experimenting": they were worried that he was substance-sniffing, which had ended up with him setting fire to the duvet of the bed next to him. They would be sending me the bill for a replacement. I was worried sick that my son had been tempted to try substance abuse, and I couldn't speak to him for another week when he had an exeat. I knew that he would not ring me, knowing he was in trouble, and I couldn't call him.

When I collected Anthony for his exeat, I asked him what was going on.

"Mum, they think I am glue sniffing, and you know how I hate that sort of thing."

"Well, what were you doing to burn Mathew's duvet?"

"We wanted to see what happened with spray deodorant and a

lighter. We were sitting on my bed and sprayed the deodorant and lit the lighter, and it worked like a flame thrower and caught Mathew's duvet on fire. We put it out quickly and it wasn't damaged much."

"What on earth were you doing with a lighter in the first place?"

"It wasn't mine, it was Greg's, and we just wanted to see what happened. No one was sniffing anything."

"Well, I have the bill for your little escapade and you will pay every penny of it."

"Okay, Mum. I'm sorry."

It was just two weeks later that he came home for the Christmas holidays. Relations had sent him money for Christmas and he offered this to pay off his debt.

"No," I said, "You can put that in your savings account. I want you to earn the money to pay this off. Go out and find baby-sitting jobs or any other paid job. I don't mind how long it takes you, but I want it paid back with your hard-earned money, not Christmas money you were given." It took him some time, but at Easter Anthony handed me £4 and said:

"This is the final payment I owe you for the duvet."

"Thank you, Darling. Now I never want to hear about this sort of nonsense again."

Anthony was a pretty normal teenager with an enquiring mind, and with his very white hair, he stood out in a crowd. He had his share of trouble at school and invariably took the brunt if there were several of them running in the passage, or whatever rule they were breaking. Anthony would always be pulled up even if the others went unrecognized. One day when I collected him for a weekend, he announced,

"I want to dye my hair brown. I am so tired of sticking out like a sore thumb."

"Oh, I do understand, but you have such beautiful hair, it would be a shame to lose it." He never did dye it, thank goodness.

Life at Toddington could not have been nicer. During the season we had shoot weekends every other weekend, and in the summer the gardens were open to the public and the rare breeds of cattle and sheep were on show in the fields. During his exeats and holidays Anthony came home, sometimes with a friend or two, but usually the Bowman Shaw boys had the same time off. During the summer holidays Justin would get a school team together and Anthony would invite boys from his school to play in a cricket match. A sumptuous tea was served at half time, and then the boys continued their match. This was usually followed by swimming in the pool while a bar-b-que was prepared for supper.

During the holidays Sir Neville employed the boys on the farm to do various jobs. One Easter Anthony creosoted the fences, which made his eyes very red and gave him a nasty rash all over his body, but he soon got over that. During the summer the boys helped with the combining: Andrew and Fergus were both old enough to drive the combines and Justin was just old enough (by a day) to drive the tractors on the road, but Anthony was still six months too young to drive. His job was to weigh the tractors and trailers that came in with the grain, and to listen to the silos up above to make sure they were not clogging. The first year Anthony did the weighing-in, I used to come up to the farm with a thermos of tea and a bun at about 6 p.m., as he started at 7 a.m. One day I arrived to find the fire brigade there and all the grain being siphoned out on to the yard. When I asked what was happening, I was told there was a fire in the drying silo, and they were trying to save as much grain as possible.

In the summer of 1985, Anthony asked me if he could go on a skiing holiday with his school. I knew it would be impossible to stretch my limited income to paying any extra on top of the school fees and his uniform—it was not just the cost of the skiing trip, he had to have money to spend while he was there and to pay for equipment and lessons. I had to say no. Anthony, however, did not give up so easily:

"But Mum, if I worked and saved up for spending money and you paid the skiing trip, would you be able to manage that?"

"Ok, that sounds reasonable—I think it might be possible." So that summer he worked on the farm, driven by his mission to save the money for his skiing trip.

One evening when he returned from work around 10 p.m., Anthony asked if he could go swimming, and I said, "That will be fine, just let me get my book and I will join you." I never let Anthony swim alone; you never knew what could happen—he could slip and crack his head open, or who knows what else. We wandered over to the swimming pool and turned the lights on, and I nestled down in a chair with my book. He dived in and swam a few lengths and then got out, saying he wanted the goggles and flippers. They were in a chest in the passageway which wasn't very well lit, so he put his hand out to switch on the light. There was a loud bang as he was thrown to the ground some distance away. I rushed over and found him very dazed—he had had an electric shock from trying to switch on the light with wet hands.

I was so angry with him that I shouted as though he were still tiny: "You should know better than touch electricity with wet hands." I think my anger was the shock that he could have been killed. I was unspeakably relieved that he was okay, but we were both very shaken and little upset.

It had been raining for days and combining had come to a standstill, so Anthony asked me if he could go and stay with his friends in Hampshire. I told him that as he had contracted to work on the farm and was being paid basic while laid off for rain, he could not leave. Instead he suggested his friends come to Toddington, and I agreed that was fine. One morning the weather had cleared and combining was beginning again, so Anthony had to telephone his friends and tell them not to come and stay. I remember telling him to hurry up, as he would be late for work. I drove him up to the farm and said goodbye. At lunchtime, I packed up sandwiches for all the boys and then drove round the various fields to find them with a cold drink and lunch, and if I wasn't too busy I would stay and have a sandwich with Anthony. This day Lady Bowman Shaw said she would take the lunches round, so in the evening, I prepared the thermos of tea and a bun at 6 p.m. to go and join Anthony for 15 minutes or so before I started back at work.

I drove up to the farm and saw the grain being siphoned out of the silo and presumed they had had another fire while drying the grain. I was asked to go and park up at the back, as the services were about to arrive. I walked down to where the manager's children were and I asked, "What has happened?"

Thomas replied, "They can't find him."

"Can't find who?"

"They can't find Anthony"

"What do you mean, they can't find Anthony?"

"He fell in the silo."

"How could he fall in the silo?!" I screamed.

"He was helping to unblock it," replied Christopher.

I learnt later that Anthony had heard the silo blocking up and he had called the manager, John, on the radio to come and unblock it. They had both gone up into the silo and John said, "I need to go down there and rod it." Anthony immediately offered to do it himself, and John, not even thinking this six-foot young man was only 15, said, "Ok, I will go down and see if it is clearing."

Anthony then went down the ladder and stood on one of the cross beams and leaned on another one above and started rodding the grain. John said he heard a scream and he came back up and then down the ladder to find Anthony in the grain. John grabbed hold of Anthony, but from the ladder on the wall he could not pull him out, as the machines in the silo were sucking him under. So he let go and went back up and out of the silo to switch it off, but when he returned Anthony was gone. He then called the Emergency services and all farm workers to come and help, and that is when I arrived, not knowing this terrible dilemma.

I flew past the children and rushed up the steps of the silo and peered down into this enormous silo with black grain near the bottom, and several of the farm workers were in the grain frantically trying to find him. In that minute of seeing this situation, I knew there was no hope for Anthony.

John put his arm on my shoulder and said, "There is nothing you can do to help here, Anna. Come back to the house and have some tea."

I remember screaming, "You have to get him out!" and I was escorted back to John's house to wait. Lady Bowman Shaw came and someone made tea, I remember wanting more Earl Grey, which was in the thermos in the car for Anthony. Someone also thought it a good idea to put sugar in it for shock. This promptly made me sick. I remember a doctor being there and being given an injection; everything seemed so surreal, like I was looking down on it happening to someone else.

I think I was very calm, but I remember saying, "It is too late; he will have suffocated in that grain." They reassured me that we must wait and not to give up hope yet, but I knew he had no chance of survival in that silo.

An hour later Lady Bowman Shaw came and put her arms around me and said they had found him.

"Is he dead?" and she nodded. We all sobbed, but again it was like looking down on someone else.

I wanted to scream the place down and hit anyone near me, but I was quite docile. I announced, "I have to go and get everything ready for the dinner party."

"There will be no dinner party, and Gay is coming home with you to stay the night," Lady Bowman Shaw assured me. It was suggested that I had a stiff drink, which someone poured me, but again it made me sick.

Every evening when Gay finished work in the office, she used to come up to my apartment and have a cup of tea with me before she left for home and I left for the farm with the thermos for Anthony. Tonight had been the same, but then she had left to go for a doctor's appointment and while waiting in the surgery she had heard the sirens and seen the doctor rushing out of the surgery, and not for one minute realizing it was an accident on the farm. When she came up to my flat on this day she had missed the mayday call on the radio for all hands to help.

We sat up and talked well into the night. I cried a lot and so did Gay. It was the worst day of my life.

I regretted that I had shouted at Anthony to hurry up that morning, and that I hadn't taken him his lunch as usual. Things were a blur for me. Bella, my best friend from my childhood, came and stayed for a few days. She helped me sort out all Anthony's clothes, and I gave her a pair of jeans, which 22 years later, she still has and wears once a year. Dear Bella—it was like we were children again, nothing seemed to have changed in our relationship. I remember telephoning her mother in Ireland to tell her that Anthony had been killed in an accident. Her mother, Elizabeth, was my mother's best friend and she was a second Mum to me as a child. She must have telephoned Bella and there she was.

Someone somehow got hold of my brother Andrew, who was in a small village in Italy with his truck broken down and waiting for it to be repaired. He left his truck and flew straight home to be with me. Although I do love my brother, we have not always seen eye to eye and the last person I wanted living in my house was Andrew, but as Lady Bowman Shaw said, I needed someone to shout at.

Someone must have telephoned my aunt, but on this terrible day—it was August 13th—I truly felt she had put a curse on Anthony, and had caused him to die. I told Andrew that I could not be alone with Lois for some time, as I would surely say something I would regret. Of course she had not caused his death: she adored Anthony despite the hard time she gave me with him as he was growing up, but I needed to blame someone. It was just too uncanny that he should be born at 6.15 p.m. on 13 February and he died around 6 p.m. on 13 August, 15 years later.

One positive thing that came out of this frightful accident was the law was changed the very next day. There had to be two people, if anyone climbed in a silo, and also harnesses had to be worn. Hopefully this would prevent the same thing happening to anyone else.

Because the accident happened in August, most people were away on holiday, including the local vicar. A temporary vicar was holding services in our local church, so I turned to Anthony's Chaplain from Lord Wandsworth College. He performed the Memorial service with the help of Anthony's House Master. It was almost fortuitous that people who knew Anthony well held the service. I arranged for three pieces of his favourite music to be played: "Sailing," which was his treasured first LP; "Don't Cry for me Argentina," which I found in his cassette player; and "Nimrod" which he loved to play in the car. Anthony had been cremated the previous day, with Andrew and I, and two friends at the short service.

Friends, relations and many people Anthony had known came to the memorial service, but several of his best friends were not there as they were away and I could not reach them. It was a beautiful service and I sobbed all the way through. It was so final—I would never see my lovely boy again. My last sight of him was at the funeral parlour where they had done the best they could for him, but what went through my mind was that I wished I could wash his hair: it was so dirty looking after his long day at work. I also wished they could get all the black rape seed oil out from between his teeth; he had such beautiful straight teeth with a lovely smile. Strange, the little details a mother thinks of her son.

After the service, the Bowman Shaws' invited all the guests to the manor for tea and it gave me the opportunity to chat to my relatives and Anthony's friends and acquaintances. Everyone was still very much in a state of shock. I was in a daze and it certainly hadn't sunk in that I would never see Anthony again; I clung to the feeling that he was only away at boarding school.

I received many letters of condolence. One was particularly poignant, from a mother of a boy who had been at school with Anthony: when he had visited the school to sit the exam, he had been given a "guardian" to show him around, and this boy had been his guardian. He was very gifted musically and was singing in a choir in Europe when he had a heart attack and died just a week or so before Anthony died. I knew I had to write to her to let her know how much her son had meant to him of his first visit to the school. Another letter I received was from one of the boys in his class and House, who had shared a dormitory with Anthony and twelve other boys: he wrote that "Anthony was very generous and always leant money." I had to smile, it came right from the heart. No one had told him what to write or corrected it.

I was so amazed at the number of letters I received from his 15-year-old friends and peers. I could never imagine writing a letter like that when I was their age: but then, I didn't lose a good friend at that age either.

Andrew moved in with me and Sir Neville found work for him on the farm. He joined the Young Farmers and at one of the meetings he met a woman named Denise, who eventually became his second wife. Andrew and I travelled down to Cookham Church with Anthony's ashes; our cousin David (Lois' eldest son), who lives in Cookham, joined us and we interred the ashes with those of our other family members. It is a very pretty church right on the river Thames, and the graveyard around the church is beautifully maintained.

I stayed on at Toddington Manor for a year, but when harvest time came round again I could not face it, and decided it was time to move on again. Life was very difficult and it was hard to adjust from being a mother for 15 years to nothing in one split second. In the morning I had taken my son to work and by the evening, I was no longer a mother. Harvest time brought it all back to me. How does one adjust to losing so much so suddenly? I didn't know the answer. I had many friends who rallied round and tried to cushion the hurt I was going through. It was hard talking to Andrew, as tears came into his eyes every time we spoke of Anthony, and that would set me off. Some days I just didn't want to get up and start the day. My body felt heavy, and I would have given anything to be left in peace, to stay in bed and sleep and never wake up. I saw no purpose in carrying on. All my life I had worked hard and strived to make a home for my little family and I had struggled so hard to keep Anthony, he was so precious to me. He was my world, and everything I worked for and achieved was for him. Now what was the purpose for living? I was 35 and had had a hysterectomy two years before, so there was no chance of any more children. I even thought of adopting but after asking around, I was told single people were not accepted as adoptive parents. Despair was not the word for it: I did not want to live. I felt I had been dealt a series of very unfair blows, losing both my parents as a child and then losing my one precious child so young.

The first Christmas without Anthony was very sad, but thankfully the Christmas dinner had to be cooked for the Bowman Shaw family. They had always invited Anthony and me to join them. I couldn't help myself thinking of what I might have got him for Christmas, I always bought him some sort of family game, which we always enjoyed playing on a Sunday evening. Gradually, I learned to try and find something nice to look forward to, and it certainly helped. I particularly made a great effort to do something interesting on any anniversary. On Anthony's first birthday after his passing, my great friend Vron invited me to see the Spanish Riding School at Wembley. This was a wonderful treat, and I realized it helped me to cope. Every first time event after his death was very difficult to cope with, and certain places brought back so much, particularly the M3 motorway, which was the route we took to school.

Those first three years after his death were very touch-and-go. I had to try and convince myself that life really was worth living. I found a job as a cook for a millionaire and his girlfriend who had bought the village of Croxton near Cambridge, but I was miserable there and so found another job, working for a princess of Ghana and her husband who had homes in London and the country. I was even more miserable at that position, and was beginning to think that I was now unemployable.

My employment agency sent me for an interview to work for royalty, Their Royal Highnesses Prince and Princess Michael of Kent. The first interview was at Kensington Palace, and then I was sent for a second interview at their country house, where I met the Prince and Princess. I arrived early and was invited into the kitchen by the cook, who gave me a cup of coffee while I waited to be summoned to meet Their Royal Highnesses. The cook kindly offered me some hints on etiquette and how the Princess liked the house run. One thing that sticks out in my mind is soft-soled shoes. Soft-soled shoes must be worn in the house, so that footsteps were not heard going up and down the stairs. I was also reminded that Their Royal Highnesses are addressed as "Good Morning, Your Royal Highness" first thing in the morning and then Ma'am or Sir during the day, and again "Goodnight, Your Royal Highness" last thing at night, or whatever salutation, depending on the time of day.

As we were chatting away, Princess Michael breezed into the kitchen, all kitted out for riding. I was so taken aback at this entrance, that I was struggling to get out of my chair and stand to address her. She said a couple of words and was gone.

Shortly afterwards the cook came and told me, "His Royal Highness will see you now. I will take you up to his study."

I was very nervous, and was shown into his study where I greeted him, "Good morning, Your Royal Highness."

"Good morning, Mrs. Murray." In a few moments he made me feel very much at ease and was perfectly charming. We chatted for about 15 minutes and then I was dismissed. The Cook informed me that the agency would let me know the next step.

I was invited to go back to the country house to spend a weekend and work to see how we all got on. A date was arranged and I duly arrived—with my soft soles—at 9 a.m. sharp. However, when I arrived, the cook greeted me:

"Did the agency not let you know this morning that the Her Royal Highness had changed her mind?"

"They couldn't possibly have done, as I stayed with cousins close by, so I could be here early. My drive from home was four hours." It was probably meant to be that I didn't get the job there, but I had fun trying. Soon after I found a job as a cook for The Earl and Countess of Inchcape in Buckinghamshire. I enjoyed it there as much as I could enjoy life. It was very civilized and I had a beautiful kitchen with an aga and my own little sitting room off the kitchen, with a television. The house had a full staff: in addition to me, there was a butleress, governess and cleaner, and of course gardening staff. My main job was to cook for the family, but I also took on the dogs, especially when the puppies arrived. I looked after them and brought them up until they were ready to leave for their new homes.

One day, the butleress asked me to drive her to an interview, as she didn't drive. We set off for Tring and arrived at the Bonsor's House, Little Stocks, in the small village of Aldbury. Mrs. Bonsor was charming and insisted that I joined them, and after the interview we were shown the cutest little cottage that would go with her job.

On the way home we were discussing the pros and cons of the job and that evening she came to me and told me that she had telephoned the Bonsors to say she couldn't take the job, as she felt it was too isolated for her because she didn't drive. The Bonsors had then asked her to ask me if I was interested, as they liked me. I returned their call and said that I was only a cook, not a cleaner, but they assured me it would only be cooking: eventually they persuaded me to take the post. It was strange, because I wasn't looking for another job at the time.

Life with the Bonsors was very pleasant, and I had plenty of riding and a lovely garden to work in, but the cleaning in the house kept creeping up and in the end I went back to my employment agency and asked them to find me a job cooking only. They arranged three interviews for me, and I decided to let the Bonsors know that I was looking elsewhere. They were so upset they said they would immediately arrange to get a cleaner, so long as I stayed. I agreed, and

decided I would go to the interviews anyway, just to give me something to do and an outing.

I was finding it very hard to go anywhere, or speak to anyone,
and I never telephoned anyone. I was having problems just coping
with everyday life, and had no idea in which direction I was going. I
was a lost soul, and very depressed. I think the person that helped me
the most was Denise, Andrew's new wife. She was born with common
sense and she was especially kind and sensitive to me, and somehow I
found I could talk to her, as she never knew Anthony. She also suggested that I contact the Bereaved Parents Association, who she had
already contacted on my behalf, but I had to make the first call to
them. Once I made that call, then they would call and check up that I
was all right and always be there for me to talk to. Well, making that
first call was one of the hardest things I have ever done. I have never
felt I needed help from anyone and always felt I could manage on my
own. I don't ever remember asking anyone for help, and I had no idea
what I was going to say. Denise kept trying to persuade me to call
them, and all I had to say was my name. I did make that call, and perhaps it was a good thing. I never called them again, but they called me
regularly to check I was okay and coping. I suppose it helped to talk
to someone who was not directly connected to Anthony but had also
been through the horror of losing a child: I did not feel so alone.

In the meantime, I was still trying to find a purpose to my life
and I went to the three interviews the agency had arranged. One was
to a Lord who lived in Calne; it wasn't what I was looking for, if I
had been looking, but was interesting none the less. The next one was
with a famous English film star, Anthony Andrews, and his family,
who were far more down to earth—again, I didn't need the job, but
enjoyed having a look.

The last interview was in Paris. An air ticket was purchased
for me, and I was met at the airport by a taxi and driven to Chantilly:
I remember thinking what a lovely wide-open space the area was. We
turned off the motorway and drove through forests on either side for
several miles, and then there it was, the beautiful Chateau of Chantilly
with the race course on the left. It was a magnificent sight, with large

gates at the bridge over the moat and the chateau behind. We drove
past it on the cobbled road and under an archway, and on the left, I
later found out, as my driver spoke no English, was the famous Musée
du Cheval, Les Grandes Ecuries (the Horse Museum). All the buildings were very old and beautiful, and the houses on each side of the
street made you feel like you had arrived in olden times. At the traffic
lights, we turned left and came out by the race course with the Grand-
stand in the distance. We drove on to Gouvieux and arrived at a solid
wooden gate; the driver pressed a bell in the wall and we were let
through. There before me was a beautiful house (which was in fact a
Mill with the river running through it), and acres of lawns and gardens
running down to the main river. To my right, as we came through the
gate, was a charming little cottage, which I later found out was to
be my cottage. I met Freddie Head and his partner Chantal. Freddie
Head had been the top jockey in France for the previous seven years;
he and Chantal had a son, Christopher, and were expecting a second
child. Freddie had two older daughters by his first wife. I was offered
a very good salary, a car and a beautiful cottage within the property.
The Heads were away for the whole of August, racing at Deauville,
and would be again for two months in the winter when they went to
the Bahamas. They expected me to stay in their house while they were
away, and I was free to invite guests to stay in my cottage. The indoor
staff consisted of an English nanny, a cleaner, a laundry lady, and
a cook.

I returned back to the airport via the Chateau of Chantilly,
which was so beautiful I fell in love with it. The racecourse lay next
to Les Grandes Ecuries. It was the most beautiful town I had ever
seen. My mind was turmoil: I had no intention of leaving my job, and
yet here I was being offered something I could hardly turn down. On
returning back to England, I rang my brother and told him where I had
been and what I had been offered.

His response was, "Take it, Anna, take it. I would have wished
for something like this a long time ago, but I think it was too soon.
Now, I think you should make a clean break and perhaps start a
new life."

For once in my life I felt comforted by these encouraging words. This was certainly going to be a challenge: I was going to have to learn a whole new language, but perhaps this was the sort of challenge I needed. I know I needed to keep myself occupied in all my waking hours. I tried very hard not to give myself time to think about me, and this maybe the opportunity I needed.

I accepted the Heads' offer and duly handed in my notice to the Bonsors, who were very sad to see me leave. I was also sad to leave them, as I had met all the family and we all got on so well.

CHAPTER 5

FRANCE

I could only take a few items of furniture as the cottage was small and furnished, although I was able to replace some of it with my own things. I put my cats into a cattery, wanting to make sure I was doing the right thing before I sent them over to France—I would not be able to bring them back without six months quarantine. After two weeks, I knew I would be staying, so Andrew shipped the cats by air, and I was as happy to see them as they were to see me.

Life was a challenge from the start. Except for the nanny, the staff spoke no English, so I had to get on and learn the language so we could communicate. The Heads arranged a tutor for us to learn the language, and I also took classes in the town twice a week in the evenings. It was interesting learning the new food, and the way the French eat, several small courses, with salad and cheese following the main course, and dessert last.

In the first few weeks when I knew no one, I took the train to Paris and visited many delightful parts of the city. My friend Bella told me she had a cousin living in Paris; we made contact and they invited me to dinner. It was a beautiful apartment on the Seine, which had a view of the Eiffel Tower filling up the enormous French window. Ben and Pat Ryan invited an Irish friend of theirs, Diana Cresswell, who was also interested in riding, and we became lifelong friends. I invited Diana to come up to Chantilly and ride with me, as I belonged to the local riding school.

A few things I really missed were playing bridge—I never thought I could play bridge in French—and English Sunday newspapers. I eventually found other interests to distract me from these longings. During that first summer in France, Bella, who lived in Scotland, informed me that her husband, John, had been diagnosed with inoperable cancer, and that they were planning a trip to France. They came over with John's brother and his wife, and I invited them all to lunch. It was a fun reunion.

On the 5th of November, I was invited to a Guy Fawkes and Fireworks party on the neighbouring farm. I was astounded to find there were so many British people in the community: I asked who had built the bonfire and was told that it was the British Scouts. I mentioned that I had been a cub scout leader in the U.K. The scout leader came over to me, introduced himself as Geoffrey Auckland, and said they were in need of a Scout leader. This was a marvelous introduction to the local English-speaking community, and so I resumed my scouting life as a scout leader. I was a little nervous at the beginning, as I had only been a cub leader to small boys up to the age of 10. The scouts were all older and, of course, doing more difficult things, which meant a lot of homework for me, planning their meetings and activities.

At Christmas, when the Heads went to their holiday home in the Bahamas, I invited my aunt Lois and a friend, and my cousin Penny and her friend Kathy from the States all over to stay. We planned a sumptuous Christmas dinner and I invited Diana and her cousin to join us. It was on Christmas day when we all got on so well that Lois suggested that Diana and I join her and go on a trip to Kenya. Well, I was so excited about this and hoped Diana would join us. I think she was sort of forced into it: I am not sure that she would have agreed to come if she had been left to her own devices. My aunt arranged everything, then asked us to send her the money for our share. We arranged to go at the end of March, which was still the rainy season in Kenya, but the prices were very expensive from April onwards. Diana paid her share and then realized she was now committed to come to Kenya with us.

This was the trip of a lifetime, and I think for Diana too. Returning to Kenya after 27 years, I saw many changes, but was also reminded what a beautiful country it is. I miss my wonderful childhood, but nothing can take away my incredible memories.

***

In June I received a phone call from Pat Ryan in Paris.

"Anna, are you seated?"

"No," I replied, "has something happened to John?"

"No," she said, "It is Edward."

"What has happened to Edward?" I asked.

"He was playing with a young friend, and they were throwing sticks (they were pretending they were spears) and one went into Edward's eye, and he is now on a life-support machine. They will be pulling the plug tonight, as he has shown no sign of life," Pat told me.

"Oh my God! Poor Bella and John! I must telephone them immediately—no, I will ring Linda, who is one of her best friends in Glasgow." I telephoned Linda, and she said they were hanging on but she would let me know the outcome. Later that evening Linda rang me to say they had turned off the life-support machine and Bella and John were still at the hospital.

"When do you think the funeral will be?" I asked.

"On Saturday. Can you come?"

It was Thursday evening and I said, "Yes, of course, I will be there. I will work on getting a flight to arrive early Saturday morning."

"Let me know what time the flight gets in to Glasgow, and I will come and meet you there." Linda replied.

All four of Bella's brothers were there with their wives and families: some of them I hadn't seen since I was 12 years old, before I left Kenya. Bella and John were so glad to see me there and I felt so sad for them, knowing what lay ahead. Bella had already lost one of her brothers, Mark, who fell in a pit and drowned in Kenya, leaving a widow and young family. This was such a sad day for all of us. Edward was eight years old and had just been invested as a Cub Scout: his whole life lay ahead of him, shot down in a split second, while playing with his friend.

I was still totally bereaved at losing Anthony and felt in no position to help Bella, John and Elizabeth: my heart was wrenched out for them. There is nothing in this world worse than losing a child, and now my best friend had lost her beloved Edward. To make matters even worse, John was dying of cancer. I could not imagine how Bella was going to cope with this overload of loss ahead of her. I really wondered whether there was a God. How could anyone endure so much and still carry on? I thought my world had come to an end when I lost Anthony, and now Bella was getting a double whammy. I just prayed that she would have the strength to cope. When I returned to France, I telephoned Bella and John regularly, to keep in touch and just chat.

In the meantime, I still had a job that I was finding rather boring. During the summer while the Heads were in Deauville, their neighbours, the Philippis, who had held the Guy Fawkes evening, had asked if I would do a dinner party for them. It had been very successful, and one of the couples invited, from the British Embassy, asked me if I would be interested in doing this sort of thing for the diplomats in Paris. They asked me to give them my details and they would circulate it in the Embassy newsletter.

Talking to various members of the English community, many encouraged me to do catering, and they would use me too, so I gave in notice to the Heads. The Philippis had a small cottage on three acres at the bottom of their farm that they were willing to rent to me for a small fee. The cottage was sweet, but so overgrown with weeds and nettles that it was almost impossible to get to the front door, hence the low rent.

Not long after I moved in, I received a phone call from a diplomat at the Embassy, asking me to do a dinner party for them. This was so successful that two of the guests asked for my telephone number and soon requests for cocktails and dinner parties were coming in from other embassies as well, where they had been at dinner parties I had done. I had business cards and menus printed, so I could send them out.

Meanwhile, Diana had been looking for somewhere to rent in the area and the Philippis offered her the apartment above their sta-

bles, again at a very low rent as it was in very bad shape and had no
heating. She was still working in Paris for an American law firm, but
wanted to find something in the area.

I never saw the flat until the day before Diana moved in: I was
there to help clean it up so we could move her furniture up the stairs
and get her settled in. My shock and horror could not be hidden. The
condition the place had been left in was appalling. There was a winding staircase and then a long passage with a door halfway along, and
there seemed to be masses of rooms—seven in fact, including the
kitchen, and at the far end of the passage was a bathroom. Every room
was full of clutter. One room had obviously been used as a bedroom:
there was a double bed which had been made into a four-poster with
rough fencing wood. Between the posts the previous occupants had
papered the walls with a totally different paper and colour from the
rest of the room. The colours and textures actually hurt my eyes.
There were dirty clothes left lying around and under the bed; once we
had got rid of it, we found a number of condoms. I could not believe
Diana had agreed to rent this place, but she said she could see the
potential under all this garbage.

We spent a whole day clearing out all the junk and bagging it
all, throwing out any furniture that Diana could find no use for and the
following day the furniture van arrived. We got her installed in one
bedroom and for the next week, the two of us painted and ripped out
wallpaper. In Diana's spare time she carried on painting: the apartment was huge and it took several weeks to get the basic rooms done.
We left the others until she had more time. She made beautiful curtains and had nice log fires in the living room and dining room. There
was plenty of free wood from the huge pile just across the drive from
her front door. Because the place was so large and had no heating, she
also bought some paraffin heaters, and kept the door half way down
the passage closed to try and keep the heat in. The flat was charming
in the summer, with window boxes filled with geraniums, but in the
winter I really took my hat off to her. I could not have lived there.

I had been talking to some of the parents of my Scouts: many
of them worked for the Aga Khan at Aiglemont, and they gave me

the name of the director of Human Resources and suggested I send in a curriculum vitae so that if any jobs became available they could contact me. I passed this information on to Diana and suggested she do the same. We were both offered jobs: she as a secretary and I in charge of the cleaning crew for the offices. This suited me very well, as my hours were from 6 a.m. until 9 a.m. and then 5 p.m. until 8 p.m., Monday to Friday. It meant I could develop my new catering business, knowing I had an income. I worked there for six months, until my business was all set up and I felt I could manage without the regular income.

I did at first wonder if I had bitten off more than I could chew. I was an English cook setting up my own business in France, and my French was still not very good. Luckily, I had great support from many in the English community, some of them married to French people and others with knowledge of accounting or of setting up a business. I gleaned all the help I could from whoever I could, and Anna's Kitchen was launched.

An English friend, Jane, who worked for the Master of Hounds, introduced me to French hunting. She took me to the hunt and we followed by car: almost immediately I was completely hooked on this sport.

We arrived at the rendezvous in the heart of the forest, and everyone was milling around chatting to each other. Jane introduced me to several people, and then the *trompes* (French horns) were blown and everyone congregated in a semi-circle around the Master of Hounds. Jane explained to me the different categories of huntsmen/women: there was the Master, Mme d'Aillières; the Huntsman, Daguet; and then the boutons, who wore navy-blue frock coats with gold and red around the collar and cuffs, and navy corduroy jodhpurs depicting the Rallye Trois Forêts. Next were the everyday huntsmen/women wearing black hunting jackets with cream, brown or white jodhpurs and then the relais, who usually wore a navy jacket and black or navy jodhpurs. The Huntsman arrived with the hounds, and four men with caps on stood in a line between the hounds and the

Master. Each in turn spoke and Jane explained to me, they were telling the Master where they had seen a stag. After they had each told
her where their stag was, she chose one of the stags, and everyone got
on their horses and they went off after the hounds, looking for this
particular stag, *trompes* blowing. This sound of the French horns in
the forests was something hard to describe, and to this day brings me
out in goose pimples and excitement. I can't tell you the thrill it gave
me to hear the *trompes* blown as the hunt moved off in the forest.

We followed by car, and got out to walk and follow on foot,
and then back to the car to carry on following the hunt. We got out
again, when someone told us the hunt was coming down through
the forest, and there before our eyes was a huge stag with enormous
antlers trotting down the hill past us: a short while later the hounds
arrived and then the horses, followed by the bikes. The crowd following was huge, so many people out to watch the hounds working. They
came by car, bike, on foot and on horseback. We heard the *trompes*
blowing again, and Jane told me that meant the stag had gone into
the water; and then a different tune was played, which meant the stag
had got out on the island. All the horses came charging past us, and
we turned round and followed on foot. The horses had to wait on this
side, except a few of the *boutons* (pronounced Bootons) who were allowed onto the island. We could hear the hounds hunting well by their
cries, and the *trompes* blew four loud blasts, and then there was shout-
ing, indicating they had seen the stag. Suddenly there was crackling in
the undergrowth, and there he was. He jumped back in the water and
swam over to our side with the hounds in hot pursuit. Out he came
and ran past us, up the hill into the forest. We realized he was probably heading for the other side of the road, so we made our way back
to the cars and out on to the main road, where people said they had
seen him cross. We actually got to the spot where the stag crossed before the hounds arrived and we watched them following the scent and
crossing the road. The horses were not too far behind. What a picture.

We then waited to see which way he might go. We were just
getting out of the car to follow on foot when we heard the *Hallali*

which was the special tune blown when the stag was at bay. Very
shortly afterwards we heard the bang when the Huntsman shot the
stag. Jane explained to me that the hounds hold the stag at bay by surrounding him: he may be lying down or standing with a glazed look,
but the hounds never touch the stag. They wait until the Huntsman ar-
rives. He has to get off his horse and put his gun together. It is broken
and housed in two sheaths either side of his saddle; he then loads it
and takes aim. Now the stag has had some time to recover himself and
sometimes takes off, and leaves everyone standing around, or he is
shot quickly.

Once he is shot, the butchers arrive in a van and take the beast
back to the rendezvous. The Master and Huntsman return with the
hounds and riders, and foot and car followers find their way back
to the rendezvous. Everyone brings something towards a picnic and
several bunches of people get together and share the food: wine is offered, or hot tea or soup.

While everyone is enjoying the picnic, the butchers skin and
then carve the good meat off the stag, leaving the stomach and offal. The head and skin are then used to cover the stomach and offal
and the Huntsman blows his *trompe* to announce the finale. Everyone
circles the stag, and the hounds are brought out and usually the person
who chose the stag will stand over the dead stag, waving the horns
and teasing the hounds until they begin howling. The *boutons*, with
some of the followers blowing *trompes*, get into three lines coming
in to the circle. Each line is two people wide, so there are maybe 24
trompe blowers. The music from those *trompes* brings tears to my
eyes. Each line plays a tune, then the next line carrying on and back
to the first line again. For different times of the year they might have
a special tune: for example the St Hubert, which is the Opening meet,
or for Christmas, or because someone from the hunt died, or whatever.
While the music is played the Master and Huntsman are chatting and
deciding who to present with *l'honneur* (the stag's hoof). They then
present l'honneur to whoever they have chosen, the stag's head and
skin are removed from the stomach and organs, and the Huntsman finally allows the hounds to eat. They charge in and tear it up: the smell

is simply ghastly. One hound might run off with the backbone, and
another will try and take it off him. The *trompes* then play again: for
me, this is the best time to leave. Leaving the forest with that lovely
sound of the horns being blown, with night falling and a chill in the
air, is the part I love most.

I helped Jane exercise the horses and then was asked to ride
a second horse out to the Master's son. This was becoming a regular event for me, and I was getting to know people at the hunt. Mme
d'Aillières, then started asking me to do dinners for her and food for
the hunt. Gradually other people involved in hunting asked me to do
dinners for them, either at country houses or in Paris. The horse train-
ers also heard about me: Chantilly is very big in racing, with two of
the top Group 1 races held on the course.

I realized this is what I needed—I had to keep busy all the
time. Work was coming in and I found it hard to turn anything down:
sometimes I did big events back to back and at times I wondered if I
would get any sleep at all. I enjoyed every minute of it and was thankful I had so much going on.

It was through Jane that I was asked to make a wedding cake
for one of her friends, and of course, I was invited to the wedding
reception. There were many friends I knew at the reception and I was
introduced to Wendy Milbank, whom I was told had been catering in
the area for years when she lived in Chantilly, but she had recently returned to live in England and was catering at the Jockey Club in Newmarket. Wendy and I got on famously, and had so much in common
with our catering. We were to become good friends and colleagues.
As she still had many contacts in the racing world in Chantilly, she
was often asked to come over to cater for weddings and large parties.
At these events she invited me to help and often made use of my prep
kitchen and also my kitchen and wait staff: I had a very good profes-
sional team of Filipinos, recruited through the British Embassy, who I
used for big events.

Wendy was an inspiration and we always had such fun working together. It was sometimes exhausting, working long hours, but

we always seemed to be able to make it fun, with plenty of laughs and great pride after another successful event. She often asked me to go over to Newmarket to help her with Gold Cup Week, where she exclusively catered for a Sheik at his Stud Farm in Newmarket. One year I was free and, with two of my best helpers, we went over to England. She had the loan of the house opposite, as they were away on holiday, and we stayed there.

A huge tent was erected on the edge of the parade ground for the stallions, with their stables behind. On the Monday evening we catered for a cocktail party for 1,500 people, mainly from the press. The food was exquisite and very attractive as only Wendy knows how to make it. The kitchen tent was enormous with about twelve of us busily erecting beautiful plates of food and keeping the delicate morsels flowing.

The following day was a buffet for about 750 VIPs, and on Wednesday there was a sit-down lobster lunch for 500. The lobsters were cooked in great cauldrons on Monday and on Tuesday, three young chaps cut them in half and removed the meat and turned them over into the other shell, giving the impression of a rounded lobster. These were then wrapped up in cling film and refrigerated until Wednesday morning, when they were unwrapped and placed on plates and mayonnaise piped on them and plates then set on the beautifully decorated tables. There were 50 tables of ten people each. It was an incredible picture.

Thursday and was another big dinner, and on Friday a special dinner for about 250 staff who worked with the horses and for the event. At the end of it all we were exhausted, but it was a pleasurable exhaustion after a very successful week.

***

One of my favourite projects was the garden. When I first moved in, the whole property was completely smothered with weeds and nettles. Diana, who has always been a very keen gardener, came and helped me. We cut down all the weeds and nettles around the house and then killed them off. In the front of the house there were two garages: one was almost falling down and the other was far too low for any car to get in. At the side of the house was a wooden gate, wide enough for a car to get through. When we tried to open it, it fell apart: reaching an area with small saplings growing amongst weeds and nettles, we found a low building with a 40-foot greenhouse abutting the house. The weeds were high and we could not see what lay ahead. In the low building we found what must have been a potting shed. I have never seen so many pots for growing plants in: there were clay pots and plastic pots in black and rusty red, all stacked inside each other. Going through the door to the greenhouse, there was a small area about ten feet square, and then another door into the main greenhouse. It was amazing, and could only be described as a Victorian greenhouse, made with wrought iron and glass and not one pane broken. Inside it was tiered with south-facing shelves starting at waist high and going up. There was also a stack of shallow trays that obviously fitted onto the shelves to hold the pots. It was an ideal spot to grow plants. There was also a heating system to prevent plants from freezing.

My first plan was to try clearing a huge area of weeds and saplings: around the edge of the area we could see there was box hedge trying to poke its way to the sunlight. It was fairly high and totally unkempt and uneven. Cutting away the weeds, we made a path down towards the river, which we could hear not far away. It was all so exciting, just like arriving in the Secret Garden. We came to a small bridge that crossed a stream: we could still hear the river ahead of us, but could see nothing as it was so overgrown. We kept cutting away a path towards what sounded like a waterfall, and came to a much larger bridge that crossed the river. At that point there was a weir, which is what sounded like a waterfall. On the other side of the bridge was a fence and we could see the Phillipi house up on the hill. Their house was about four miles away by road, but from where we were standing it was no more than a mile away as the crow flies. We both flopped

First view of the garden, nettles and weeds neck high, showing washing line going from one garage to the other, one on left we eventually pushed down.

Potting shed and Victorian greenhouse with box hedge in front.

View of garage we kept and looking through to rest of garden, after we killed the
weeds

Vegetable garden, in front of greenhouse

Island from the bridge.

View of river from the bridge

down on the bridge and dangled our legs over the side, looking at the lovely view down the river. There was a mill and wheel in the far distance. We realized then that we had just crossed an island, and it all seemed to be on my property.

I said to Diana, "This would be an ideal spot for the Scouts to do some of their activities. There is water, and perhaps they could do outdoor cooking and the island is big enough to hold about ten six-man tents—but first we have to get the area cleared."

At the next Scout Leaders meeting, I suggested we could use this land for scout activities, instead of being indoors in a hall every meeting, and that it would give the Scouts a project to help clear the land. This was agreed upon, and the Scouts and I, with Diana's help, cleared all the dead weeds. We were left with the saplings, some nearly six feet high, others only one foot high. We found a small brick wall about a foot high surrounding a tree, which in the spring we found to be forsythia; when we reached the far box hedge, found there was another hedge about two feet away, making a path, but there were saplings growing in the path too, some of which were quite large ones. The land seemed to continue on forever, and we chopped down all the weeds and came to yet another box hedge, and in the end we found three 100-foot square areas surrounded by box hedge. It must have been a beautiful garden in its heyday.

It was a Saturday in early February that an ideal opportunity arose to get rid of the dilapidated garage. I had a dinner party for 22 people at the Gate House of the British Embassy, for the Head of Chancery. Usually on Saturdays, I ran the Scout meeting but on this day I had to arrange for someone else to take over, as I had to be in Paris for the dinner party. The scouts were going to do outdoor cooking at my place, and they all arrived as I was packing up the van to go to Paris. They rushed over to the island, with their adult leader in tow, and found the necessary wood to build their fires, but it wasn't long before they came back and found me and asked if it was alright to come off the island and try and build their fires this side, in my garden. The wind had got up and it was impossible to light their fires.

Eventually, they asked if they could light one fire in the strange little lopsided garage, to try and get out of the wind. I agreed, but told them to watch out for the tall poplar behind them, as it seemed to be bending over so much in the wind. I was about to leave for Paris when we heard an enormous bang: a huge tree had fallen across the road, the road I was going to use to go to Paris. We decided to abandon the fire lighting project; instead I found saws for the boys and an electric saw for the leader, and suggested they go and try and clear the road.

Time was rushing by, and I had to leave for Paris, so I turned left and decided I would take another route. The wind was really raging by now and I found trees down everywhere, blocking my passage. I had to keep turning back and trying another road. Eventually, by finding some side roads, I reached the main road in Lamorlaye and headed towards Chantilly. As I left Chantilly I found the main road completely blocked with several trees as I approached the forest. So again, I had to turn back and I went back towards Lamorlaye again, and all seemed to be clear until I was at the top of the hill just leaving the village. There was an enormous tree right across the road. I thought of going back a short way and taking the road to Coye-la-forêt, but it was all through the forests and I was sure the road would be blocked, so I gingerly approached the fallen tree and decided to try and go through the very top of the tree which was on the edge of the verge of the road. There were leafy thin branches and I pushed my way through to the other side, and drove back on to the road and carried on my way to Paris with no further mishaps until I reached the Embassy.

I arrived at the entrance to the British Embassy and pressed the bell on the big gate. I know the guards can see my car on close circuit television, as I have seen it in their little office, but today nobody came to open the gate. I was getting very nervous, as I was already very late with my circuitous route. There was the kitchen I was supposed to be in, right above me, and I was stuck out on rue Faubourg St Honoré. I began to panic: a gendarme came up to my car and asked where I was going, and I almost screamed at him that I had a dinner in the car and had to get in there to cook it. He told me to sit on my horn until they opened the gate, so I did as I was told. The French people love to honk their horns at every opportunity; I hate it, but on this occasion I decided to do this, as I was now becoming desperate. Eventually a frazzled guard came to the gate and opened it up for me.

"What is going on? I have been sitting out there for ages, and I need to be cooking this dinner before the guests arrive," I asked.

He replied, "and we have lost half the roof on the Embassy, we had an emergency."

I asked, "Did you have that terrific storm that blew trees down everywhere in our area?"

"Did you not hear the news? Cars were being blown off the Périphérique and pillars were blown over, and the Embassy has lost a lot of its roof."

"I thought it was just in our area—I had no idea you were going through the same thing. I heard nothing, my radio is broken, and was wondering what had hit us."

When I finally managed to cook the dinner it turned out to be a success, albeit a bit late; however, the guests were delayed too, and I heard all sorts of tales about how the storm had affected different guests.

The following day, when I looked outside, I saw the tree I was worried about had also fallen, bringing another one with it. Luckily it fell away from the house and was not going to affect the garden. Diana and Gill came over and we looked at the forlorn garage and I said,

"If we stand on this side and give it a little push, I bet it will just fall to the ground." We did this, and crash went the garage as it fell in a heap. "Well, that's sorted out that problem," I said. "It was such an eye sore, I am sure no one is going to miss it."

We burnt the remains of the garage, and after the storm we heard that the Phillipis lost an enormous number of trees, so I suggested we plant some of the saplings that we were going to take up and make a lawn. We made it a project for the scouts, showing them how to dig up a sapling without damaging the roots, and then we took the trees over the Phillipi's farm and replanted them. It took us about two weeks to dig up all the saplings; then cleared the stones and eventually we rolled the ground and planted grass seed, in front of the house and by the greenhouse.

Next we tackled the second parterre, having decided to make it a vegetable garden. First we had to get rid of the saplings, and then we rented a rotovator. It was such hard work that we decided to take turns using it. We each worked it as long as we could, and then lay down on the ground to recover and the other took over. I have never felt such physical exhaustion. To make matters worse, the root system was horribly tangled: we then realized it must have been a raspberry bed which we were tearing up. Eventually we achieved a large area of well-ploughed land that we could use to grow beans, lettuces, tomatoes, carrots and cabbages and broccoli. We had a wonderful crop of vegetables that summer. It was so soothing going out into the garden to weed and water the plants and watch the vegetables grow. The lawn also was very respectable by the summer, and I took great pride in mowing it. Diana potted around the flowerbeds and when they bloomed they were amazing, so full of colour and textures. She suggested that we cut back the box hedge to its lowest level and let it grow back in a more uniform way. I couldn't believe how awful it looked and was horrified at the result, but she assured me it would grow back and would look wonderful the next year: she was right.

My days were very full with working and keeping the garden going once we had done all the basic clearing and planting, but the endeavour was a great pleasure. I realized that filling my day and keeping busy until I dropped was what I needed to keep myself sane and not fall into deep depression. I was quite successful at this and sometimes took on more than I could physically handle, but by then I knew I had to always keep busy. I did not want any time free to sit and dwell on what I had lost. I still had some very black days, which usually occurred in August around the anniversary of Anthony's death; often business was very quiet then, as most people were

away on vacation. Sometimes the despair in August was terrible and
I became quite antisocial and spoke to no one, just praying I would
get through this period and longing for September when everything
started up again.

I then decided we must have some chickens and ducks, and
I bought two female geese, naming them Harriette and Charlotte. At
night they lived in the greenhouse and perched on the tiers, safe from
the foxes. If I was out or late shutting them up, I would find everyone
tucked up in bed and I would just shut the door for the night, they
were so well trained. Harriette and Charlotte were particularly tame
and used to march into the kitchen a demand attention or food. The
noise of their honking in my kitchen was mind-blowing. We often sat
outside on the lawn for tea and the two of them would come and sit by
me, just like dogs, and Harriette was very happy to be picked up and
sat on my lap.

An American friend of mine came to the Agricultural Show
in Paris with me, and she bought a rare breed chicken egg and took
it home to incubate. She also had a habit of buying eggs at the market on Wednesdays or Saturdays, and incubating a few of those too.
Unfortunately, she lived in a built up area that did not allow chickens
and farm animals. When they hatched, a lot of the eggs proved to be
roosters: the rare breed egg was the most beautiful tiny little rooster,
red, black and white, and he only grew to about 7 or 8 inches high. He
was a real miniature, except for his voice: when he started crowing he
was so loud that she had to do something about it.

She rang me up one day and said, "I am bringing round a
present for you." When she arrived she opened up a cardboard box
and inside were four roosters, three large ones and the miniature one.
Well, I had plenty of space for them and only one rooster, so I accepted them. Everyone seemed to get on well, but the little rooster became
ferocious. He attacked me when I went into the garden to hang out
the washing, when I went into the potting shed to get food for them,
and when I went to fill up their water containers. I told my friend, "I
am going to wring his neck one of these days, he is so vicious." She

amazed me; she went right over to him, picked him up around the neck and wrung it, and then she threw him in the dustbin! I couldn't believe she had done that, and I felt rather sad, because he was a magnificent specimen, just totally vicious for such a small creature. Well, life had to go on and I couldn't dwell on his demise.

One day, when I came down the stairs into the garden, I found a large grey bird sitting there. I had no idea what it was. It didn't have feathers but grey fluff. I called a friend over and asked her what she thought it was, and she said it was a cygnet, a baby swan. We shooed it down to the river and hoped it would find its parents. A little later in the day, I found it back near my steps again. So I rang the vet and asked what I should feed it, and they said the same food as the geese and ducks, so I made a meal for it and gave it some grain and a bowl of water. It took over my front lawn, and I put a wooden box close to it so it could shelter in bad weather if needed. With the help of some friends we dug out a pond on my lawn and used a liner and filled it with water. The swan was very happy with this new arrangement. I found one of my cats sleeping on the box with the swan resting inside. All the animals seemed to accept each other: Jicky the dog, the cats, geese, ducks and chickens and the swan. One day the swan wasn't there and I became worried, and very sad that he had gone. I was in the garden lying on a lounger reading my book, *Jericho* by David Niven, and I heard a ploof, ploof, ploof coming round the corner, and there was the swan.

I shrieked, "Jericho, that is what we will call you! Oh, Jericho, I am so pleased to see you!" Jericho grew and grew and then he moved to the other lawn in front of the greenhouse, and then gradually he moved towards the river.

One day I was driving back from the village and I saw a duck in the road. There was nowhere for it to go, as all the houses had high walls and gates, so I stopped my car and caught it, and put it in my car and took it home. It was not a very pretty duck, a muscovey, but I didn't care. Diana was there, doing some gardening, and I said, "Come and have a look at what I have found."

Jericho and Puddleduck

"What?"

"I have found Puddleduck," and that is what she became known as. I took her to where Jericho was and they became firm friends. Eventually they moved to the river, only coming ashore to sleep and feed. Jericho started to lose his grey fluff and lovely white feathers emerged, and the pair of them were often seen swimming in the river, but they always appeared for food and usually slept on the bank.

One day I heard a terrible noise at the river and when I went down to explore, I found a huge yellow digger scooping out the silt from the bottom of the river and dumping it on the river bank. It was so sad: I never saw Jericho again. He must have been frightened away by this monstrosity. Puddleduck was still there, but not for long; she disappeared soon after that. I was very sad to lose them both.

***

I was asked to do a 40th birthday party in Provence, and I travelled down there with Gill, who had taken over my job at Freddie Head's. It was a black-tie affair but they had asked me to cook for the weekend. There were 20 for dinner on the night of the party, and then snacks and breakfast at 3 a.m. for up to 100 people. I was asked to bring plastic wine, champagne and water glasses, plastic plates and cutlery to cater for this number. I was a little taken aback by this request, until we arrived there and found that in fact they did not have the water facilities to cater for that number. The only water supply came from a well: when the guests arrived there were notices asking the gentlemen to use the trees, and by midnight the ladies were asked to use the trees also—no water!

We arrived on Thursday evening, after a 10-hour drive from Chantilly, and Peter, the host, had requested Guinea Fowl, which we were going to buy at the local market; but by the time we arrived he had changed his mind and asked if we could make a bouillabaisse. We looked up in a recipe all the different types of fish we needed for this and planned a trip to Marseille at 5 a.m. on Saturday morning. We arrived in Marseille at about 6 a.m., and waited on the dock for the boats to come in. We had a cold box in the car and when the first boat came in we asked if they had any of the fish we required. He gave us what we needed and told us the next boat in would have one of the other fish. In the end we bought everything we needed and put them in the cold box for our trip back. There is nothing fresher than newly-caught fish, straight out of the sea: it was a most interesting morning. When we arrived back and unpacked our shopping, we opened the cold box and were startled to find that some of the fish had tried to eat each other. The tails were poking out of the mouths of some of the fish. What a sight!

The recipe had warned that certain of the fish were deadly poisonous and not to touch them; when cooked, these actually disintegrated, but the tricky thing was trying to remember which fish were the ones we mustn't touch—it was their spines which were deadly only to the touch, once cooked they were perfectly safe. We did alright, though; the dinner was a great success and there were no fish-related mishaps. After we cooked the breakfast at 2 a.m., we tried to wash up the dishes but there was no water left: we had no choice but to leave everything until the morning, when the well would be replenished. We came away with some incredible memories of that weekend. It was a beautiful place—they had a swimming pool as well, and I've often wondered how they filled it, with water being so scarce. I will always remember the lack of water—Gill will always remember the flies.

She said, "I can't work with all these flies on every surface!"

"Well, we don't have much of an option. The owners aren't dead yet, and they live with them all the time." I replied. There was no basic hygiene.

***

One event that I will never forget was the dinner party for the Air Defense Attaché. Forty people were coming to dinner and I was cooking salmon: I had bought the salmon whole and then filleted them into 5lb fillets and packed them into an ice box. I left them by the steps so they could be put in the van last. We arrived in Paris a little early and I suddenly thought of the salmon.

"Can you see the box of salmon in the back?" I asked Gill.

She looked in the back, and said, "No, I can't see it anywhere."

"Oh my gosh," I said, "Are you sure?"

"No, it's not there."

I stopped the car and went to take a look for myself. I couldn't see it either. My heart started racing: it was a Monday and no fishmonger was open on a Monday.

I said, "We'll have to go to the Carfour (a Paris hypermarket, about four blocks from the Air Defence Attaché's apartment) and see if I can buy some there."

I drove as fast as Paris traffic allowed to the Carfour; we parked and ran into the store. I found fresh salmon, and at this stage I was prepared to pay for filleted salmon, but no luck—there was none available. The salmon was much smaller than those I had originally prepared, so instead of two large ones I bought four smaller ones, which was twice the work I had already done, but I had no choice. I bought it quickly and we arrived at the Air Defense Attaché's apartment more or less on time, but I now had to fillet all these salmon and it didn't leave much time to do the rest of the meal. Luckily Gill was a very good cook, and between us we got the show on the road; the Air Defense Attaché and his wife never even realized the terrible dilemma I had been in.

***

In 1990 I celebrated a "big" birthday, and many of my friends and relations from England and France came to join me. I invited Geoffrey Auckland and his wife Françoise, on the condition that he did not mention the scouts—he used every opportunity, where there was a crowd, to try and recruit leaders. I told him this was not the place, but he just couldn't resist reading out a poem that he had written; eventually I had it framed and now hangs in my kitchen.

An Ode to Anna the Great

This is the story of Anna the Great
when she reached the multiple of five times eight.

No-one knew of her whereabouts,
apart from her friends and some boys called Sc....(scouts)

She was, in fact, in a corner of France,
leading them all a merry old dance.

She was much loved and greatly admired,
always helping and never tired.

They loved to sample her 'haute cuisine',
English and French and a bit in between.

Her lunches and dinners were awfully good,
they fell over themselves for her 'Summer Pud'.

She lived for horses and also for cats,
she loved the races and her fancy hats!

Legend has told of her supply of coke,
and the fact that she liked an occasional smoke!

She used to pretend that she loved to camp,
except if the weather was hot, cold or damp!

I could tell you more, but you'll have to wait,
for the rest of the tale of Anna the Great.

With more and more work coming in, I decided it was time

to buy a proper vehicle to deliver my food—a saloon car was not at all suitable. I ordered a very nice van, with a back door that opened up and would help protect the food while unloading when it rained. I was so pleased with my new van and was planning on having Anna's Kitchen printed on it. I had only had it three months when I was preparing a large dinner for the Air Defense Attaché in Autuille: his apartment was on the 7th floor and one could see the racecourse from their windows. I had arrived early and parked just below the apartment, as there was a lot of preparation to be done. Before all the guests arrived, I returned to my car to bring up more soft drinks, and I found someone had been tampering with the lock—in fact they had removed it, and I couldn't open the passenger door. I had to hurry, so I picked up the sodas and returned to the apartment. After dinner, when all the guests moved to the living room, I looked out of the window and my van wasn't there. It had been stolen: it wasn't found for another year. Luckily with insurance I was able to buy another one, but did not risk a brand new one again.

One particularly memorable meal was for the Head of Chancery. It was a special lunch with the British Ambassador, the British Home Secretary, and the French Minister of the Interior. I had a table of eight in the main dining room, and in the library there was a table of six for other diplomats and minders. The host wasn't there when I arrived, but showed up a few minutes before the Ambassador arrived. Everything was prepared for them and the diplomats had told me everything must be precisely timed, as the Minister of the Interior was on a very tight schedule. He would arrive at one o'clock, and at ten minutes past they were to sit down to the first course, which was lobster bisque. I brought my own heating trolley to keep the food hot, as most of the kitchens I worked in were normal household kitchens.

Everything was going to plan: the vegetables were cooking and I was just searing off the lamb chops to go with Reform sauce when I felt a drip from above. I looked up and saw water dripping off the light fixture in the ceiling, and almost immediately the power went out. Luckily it was during the day, so I was not in darkness, but I was cooking by electricity and my heating trolley was on electricity.

I called one of the diplomats and told him the situation; they then had to try and find both the fuse box and the source of the water, which seemed to be coming from the apartment above. The host had only been living there for a week or two and had no idea where the fuse box was. I told them I could only keep the food hot for a very short time, but luckily everything was almost cooked now. I popped the lamb chops in the still-hot oven to try and finish them off. I asked if everyone could be gathered in the dining room as soon as the Minister arrived if it was at all possible, so the food could be served while it was still hot. I don't know how we pulled it off, but between the diplomats, the minders and myself, we got them into the dining room and eating their lunch—perhaps a few minutes earlier than was planned. After the lunch the host's wife arrived and I told her what had happened, and her husband came in and thanked us for keeping the show on the road.

***

I kept in touch with Bella by calling her in Glasgow. I knew she was going through a very trying time nursing John, who was now very sick with cancer. I telephoned one day and John answered, saying,

"Anna, it's so good to hear from you. When are we going to see you?" Well, I knew I was planning on going to his funeral, but realized this was ridiculous; I had to go and see John before he died. I replied,

"Can I come on Friday? I would love to see you all." He was so thrilled, he said,

"I will get tickets for the opera on Friday. Please arrive in time for the evening performance."

I then arranged to get my air ticket to Glasgow. I found a cheap flight from Beauvais to Lydd and then I would catch a coach to Heathrow, and take a flight to Glasgow, which was being offered as a return for the price of a single. The first war in Iraq had begun and everyone was scared of flying, particularly the British: they were trying to encourage people to use the airlines.

I woke up on Friday morning to hear the radio announce that all airports were closed in Southern England and Northern France due to snow. I rang Beuavais, which was a small airport, but got no reply; I then rang Lydd, but again, they didn't pick up. Eventually I rang Charles de Gaulle airport, knowing that the flight to Scotland leaves around 7 a.m., and it was 9 a.m. already. I was told they would hold the plane for me, as the runways were just being cleared and the plane had not left for Glasgow. I eventually got to the airport at 11 a.m. and was taken straight to the plane, which then took off.

I arrived in Glasgow around 12.30 p.m., but was not expected until about three o'clock. I found John at home alone and had an opportunity to chat to him before Bella returned. He was very sick and I couldn't imagine how he was going to manage going to the opera in the evening, but he cheerfully said,

"No problem, Anna, I am looking forward to it."

John struggled into the auditorium that evening, and we could see he was suffering greatly but he kept smiling and laughing. His sister and brother-in-law were also there for the weekend, to give Bella a small break from the constant nursing.

On Saturday morning Bella and her daughter, Elizabeth, and I joined Linda and her children and we went tobogganing on the hills. It was such fun and we behaved like children, every one of us. Bella and I flopped in the snow with our legs and arms outstretched and lay there looking up at the blue sky, and we chatted about everything, totally relaxed and enjoying the fresh snow air. Poor Bella, she had had so much on her plate since Edward died that it was very refreshing for her to unwind for a few moments.

A few weeks later I heard the sad news that John had passed away, and I was so thankful I had decided to go and see him before he died. I hope it meant more to him than being at his funeral. Bella and her daughter Elizabeth had a very tough time ahead of them. We lived so far apart, but I think we always felt that we were there for each other. Many a time we have had the same feelings and we know about the silences. When the worst periods have passed, we can then talk about it to each other: we both understand these very bleak periods, as we both suffered them.

***

Scouting was a great help, being physically involved with camping and various activities, and even normal meetings. My garden became a favourite for camping, where the Scouts could actually camp alone, yet I was at hand if required. Camping without an adult was one of the requirements for the camping badge, and everyone felt safe knowing the children were not going to encounter outside intruders even though they had to get on with it on their own.

The Queen came to France to open the Arche de la Défense, in Paris, and we organized to take all the Cubs and Scouts to meet her. This was very exciting for all of us. The Scouts were allowed to line the pathway that the Queen and Prince Phillip would take. They stopped and chatted to the boys and girls on their route through to meet the dignitaries of Paris. It was a memorable day for us all.

The British Scouts in Western Europe raised funds for the Children's Society, sponsored by Richard Branson, when the Chunnel was opened. Many celebrities walked the 27 miles from France to England, including the Chief Scout. The day before the Big Walk, I woke early and finished packing my bags. I had been chosen to go to Calais and present the Chief Scout with the cheque from Western Europe, which he would add to the contributions he received for participating in the walk through the Chunnel. I arrived in Calais during the late afternoon and found my way to the Hotel where we were staying. I saw several Scout members I knew and also the Chief Scout, to whom I was introduced. I felt so honoured that I would be presenting

Handing cheque to Chief Scout at entrance to Chunnel,
Calais

La Defense, to meet the Queen, Anna and Jenny

La Defense, b - Mary Pease, Jenny, Claire Belk, Anna f
-Catherine Pease, Bekky Belk, Abbie Belk and Tottie

Richard Branson at the entrance to the Chunnel, about to
start the walk through to England.

him with the cheque from the British Scouts in Western Europe. Early next morning after breakfast we made our way to the entrance of the Chunnel where there were crowds of people and press. A platform had been erected with a backdrop depicting the Children's Society, and Richard Branson was chatting to children and some well known television and sports celebrities. I was called over to the entrance of the Chunnel and invited to hand over the cheque to the Chief Scout. Photographers everywhere snapped their cameras, and then the Chief Scout joined the other celebrities ready for the start. Richard Branson gave a speech and then announced "We are off!" Everyone waved as the walkers started their 27-mile walk under the English Channel. It was quite a historical event. Shortly after this the Chunnel was opened to the public.

Two events happened every year. The first was around the 4th August, when the British Scouts joined other Associations to light the Flame of the Unknown Soldier under the Arc de Triomphe. The gendarmes brought the traffic to a halt, and we marched up the Champs Élysées to the Arc. Usually one of the Scouts had the honour of lighting the flame.

The other event in which we always participated was the Armistice Day Service on 11th November, at Cathédrale Notre Dame in Paris. We took this opportunity of investing new Cubs and Scouts in the garden behind the cathedral, after the service.

***

Geoffrey Auckland, the District Commissioner for the British Scouts in Western Europe, rang me.

"The Venture scouts are planning a trip this summer called Euroventure, where 4,500 Venture scouts will leave Gilwell Park in coaches for unknown destinations. They will be split up into groups travelling to Germany, Holland and Belgium, and after three days, everyone will come to Paris for three days."

"And you want help with the scouts when they are in Paris?" I asked.

"Well, actually, they are looking for a caterer for 4,500 scouts for the days they are in Paris. They will be camping at La Bourget airport and they are looking at setting up kitchens over the site, selling burgers, bangers, hot dogs, crisps, drinks, etc., for hungry teenagers."

It sounds strange, but I had never cooked burgers and chips before. If Anthony wanted chips, I bought 'oven chips'—this was not my type of catering. Between the top brass at Gilwell and Geoffrey Auckland they somehow persuaded me to take on this project in the name of Scouting. It was a major production, and took several weeks of planning and arranging to hire mobile kitchens and equipment. I hired my brother to come over from the UK with local burgers and bangers, and I hired a huge articulated lorry which was half fridge and half freezer, for him to drive. Andrew drove the truck to the local Metro, where I did all the shopping for the event. I had to hire masses of staff who worked all night, as the teenagers were up most of the night and then off to Paris and Euro Disney during the day. I hired three mobile kitchens: the largest one was attached to a huge tent which sat 600, the other two made their way around the site with several smaller kitchens in tents. Andrew drove around to each kitchen keeping it supplied with burgers, buns, bangers, chicken, chips, etc.

My biggest problem was that the organizers kept asking me if I had enough food: I lost count of the times I was told "you will need more than that for these chaps." The first night, we were welcome sight for the weary travellers, as there was nowhere for them to go except come to us for food; but the second night was after they had been to Euro Disney, and a lot of them stayed on and ate there. The third night they returned from a day in Paris and again many stayed on to eat in the city. My sales were nothing like the organizers had said they would be—not only that, as they were leaving on Saturday morning I was left with a large lorry full of perishable items.

It was in August: everyone was away, and I knew no customers who wanted boxes of hamburgers or bangers or even chicken pieces. I kept the truck on so I could store everything, but I had to hire a driver as Andrew had to return back to UK. I filled my freezers and fridges to capacity but I was still left with piles of food. I telephoned around the English community and told them what I had, if anyone was interested in buying anything, they could have it at cost or less—I just needed to off load everything. Panic set in, particularly when everything I had paid for on my credit card went through and there wasn't enough money in the bank to cover all the expenses. I hadn't slept properly for several days before the scouts arrived, never mind the whole week they were there. I was 65,000F short and the bank would not pay the bill for the hire of the kitchens, which was 62,000F. I still had a truck load of food and time was running out.

Someone from the church told me about several retreats that would take some of the stuff, if I could drive it up there. I ended up driving around to different parts of the Oise (the area we lived in) and giving burgers, ice-cream, bangers, and bags of chips to various retreats. I knew if I couldn't find a home for it all, I was going to send the driver back with his truck for him to dump it all or keep or sell it. At this stage I would rather it went to a worthy cause than was dumped.

I had cases of sodas stashed in my potting shed and my poor prep kitchen was loaded down with stuff I would never use: ketchup, HP sauce, barrels of frying oil, burger buns by the box load, paper cups, long-life milk and instant coffee. I made a list of everything I had left and we circulated the list to our local English-speaking community and also those at Maisons Lafitte. My freezers were full of chicken pieces, bangers and burgers, and I let the chips go.

This was one of the most stressful periods of my life. The bank took away my credit card and cheque book, and I made an arrangement to pay the kitchen hire people 1,000F a month until I had settled their bill. Life became very hard as I had to go to the bank and draw money out before I could buy any food for dinners or receptions. When my regular clients learnt what had happened, they very kindly paid half up front, which helped the cash flow.

After this frightful event, I felt I had to work even harder to try and pay back the kitchen hire as soon as possible, as the bank had promised me my credit card and cheque book once they had a note from the hirers to say I had paid them off. This wasn't easy, living in a cash-only world, and eventually I had to file for bankruptcy.

Financially life was very hard for a year, but fortunately I did not own the house I lived in nor the prep kitchen Andrew had built for me in the stables below, so they couldn't take that away from me. My assets were my clients and they could not be forfeited. I became very run down, but I continued to work and ride as ever before.

***

I became very involved with the hunting in France. Most Tuesdays and sometimes on a Saturday, I would ride a second horse for Jean-Charles Morin, a bouton with the Rallye Trois Forêts. It was a difficult clique to get into and took me years to be accepted. It was a very expensive hobby and I knew I would never be able to afford to hunt, but this was as good as hunting, and I enjoyed it enormously.

On New Year's Eve I had catered for a party for one of the boutons at the hunt, and he had said he would settle up at the hunt in two days. It was a snowy, icy day when I arrived at the rendezvous in Ermenonville, and they announced they would be moving to Chantilly as it was flatter—fewer hills might mean less ice. However, when I arrived at the new rendezvous in Chantilly it was still very icy, so I decided not to ride. I found Jean-Pierre, and went back to my van to get the invoice for the New Year's Eve dinner. As I approached my van I slipped on the ice and crashed down, putting my arm out to save me. I heard a crack and felt the pain sear through my body. I was helped up and when I saw my right arm, I realized my wrist must be broken and the middle finger was misshapen. I was taken to the emergency room to have my wrist and finger plastered in green. When we returned to the hunt, everyone was asking if I had fallen from my horse: I was dressed in hunting gear, so everyone assumed that I had taken a fall. They never guessed that I had decided not to ride anyway.

1996 Anna hunting with Jean-Charles Morin, in the Forets d'Ermononville

1999 - Last St Hubert of the Century, with five other hunts, at the Chateau de Compiegne, Anna with her beloved Erie

A broken wrist made my work very difficult, I had to learn to use my left hand to peel potatoes and work in the kitchen, and I couldn't ride. In church on Sunday, Helen Lewin came and sat beside me. She was a shy person with two boys who she tried to get to join the cubs and scouts but they were not interested. Several times, when we met up, she had asked me about riding. I wasn't too sure of her experience—many people say they ride until you put them on a horse with character and they have an awful experience. This Sunday I decided there was no harm in asking her if she wanted to come and ride Jean-Charles's horses, as I knew they would not be ridden between hunts.

I whispered to her in church, "Would you like to come and try Jean-Charles's horses?" Her face lit up and said she would love to. We arranged to meet the next morning and drove together to Ermononville, where his family had once owned the chateau there, but Jean-Charles lived with his wife and family in the old stables which were converted into a retirement home, and his brother, Gilles, (also a bouton) lived in the orangery, on the other side of the chateau, where he ran a home for handicapped. The chateau was now run as a hotel.

I decided Uselin was the best horse for her to try, as he was such a sweetie and would do her no harm. He was very fast, but boy he did have brakes! We saddled up and set off along the road with Jicky, Flax (Helen's dog) and me following. I gave her instructions on a good ride in the forest and crossed my fingers, hoping she would not get lost. The dogs and I continued at a slower pace, and about an hour later Helen and Uselin caught up with us and she announced that she had had a wonderful ride. I was so relieved that she really could ride! She was even eager to ride the other horse, which is what I usually did, taking one out after the other.

I introduced her to Jean-Charles and his wife Anna, and said that Helen would come and exercise them instead of me. Helen was even keen to do the relay at the hunt, which was great for Jean-Charles.

Every Christmas our local English church held a *Kermesse*, which was a Christmas fête, and I always saw Helen in charge of the cake stall, many of which she had made herself—she also made many of the handicrafts. Having been successful with the riding, I gingerly asked her if she would be interested in coming and giving me hand with some cooking. She was delighted, as her boys were now at boarding school in England and she would love something to occupy her days.

She was a real pleasure to work with and so thorough in her cooking and presentation, and I knew I could send her to do dinners for me knowing she would do a good job.

"Do you think that over-using my left hand is tiring it out? I am really struggling to peel these potatoes." I asked Helen, and she replied

"Yes, it could be; your left hand is not used to be worked so hard, as you are right handed."

Helen drove me to the hunt so I could follow on foot. We took her Welsh spaniel *Flax*, who loved coming to the hunt. We were at Ermenonville and the hounds and horses charged up the hill behind the old zoo. No cars were allowed up there, so we followed on foot. I struggled to walk up the hill: I couldn't believe how hard it was for me.

"Don't tell me that because I broke my right wrist, my legs won't work?" Helen laughed and said,

"Hold onto Flax, she will pull you up the hill." I was exhausted and couldn't understand why a broken wrist would make me so tired.

I was very tired when I got home, and in the next few days struggled to get my work done. By the end of the week I could hardly get out of bed, so I rang for a doctor's appointment and only got out of bed when it was time to go for the appointment. The doctor sent me for blood tests and I went home to bed. He then called me later in the day and asked me to go back to see him. I dragged myself out of bed again, back to the doctor's office, only to be told to go back to bed for the weekend and check into the hospital at 8 a.m. on Monday morning for tests. I was to do nothing: he couldn't believe I could even drive to the surgery, my blood iron level was so low.

After tests in the hospital, it was found I had pernicious anaemia, and I was started on vitamin B12 injections once a day and sent home. I was so weak and unable to cope on my own at home, so I was admitted to a convalescent home for one month. I had my blood tested regularly and also had the plaster removed from my arm and started physiotherapy while in the convalescent home. It was hard convalescing, as my customers still wanted dinners and meals, so the home became my office and I sent Helen to do all my jobs. She also took my dog home with her and we arranged for someone to feed the cats, chickens and ducks daily. Mme d'Allières, for whom I supplied soup twice a week, came to visit me and said she couldn't wait for me to recover, as her *femme de manage* (daily housekeeper) did not make soup as I did.

At the age of 79, my aunt Lois had sold up her house in England and moved out to Kenya. She bought a cute little two-bedroom, two-bath cottage at a retirement estate near Nairobi, where she had her own kitchen and had a choice of cooking for herself or going to the main house for meals. It was an ideal situation for her, and she was thrilled to be living back in the warm African climate.

When she heard of my bout of pernicious anaemia and the broken wrist she insisted that I come out to Kenya for a holiday to recuperate. It was a wonderful idea and Jane was delighted when I asked her to come with me. We booked the flight to leave on the day I was discharged from the convalescent home: my blood was now normal and I would need B12 injections just once a week.

I had made many friends in the convalescent home, and so said my farewells to everyone before Diana drove me home to pack for my trip to Kenya. I was still very weak and could not carry any heavy weight with my right arm. The flight left at midnight and we planned to leave for the airport at 8 p.m. Jane came round to my house, as Diana was driving us both to the airport. Whether it was excitement or because I was overwhelmed with all the activity, I became very ill with an upset stomach and nausea. We thought we were going to have to cancel the trip, but in the end all seemed calm: and we took a towel and paper bags in case of a recurrence and made our way to Charles de Gaulle Airport. I was so thankful to have Jane with me, as I would not have been able to do the trip without her help and encouragement—I was so weak, and ready to go home and call it a day. She helped carry the luggage and encouraged me to keep going; we would soon be in our seats and could then relax until we reached Kenya. This was the trip of a lifetime for her and I was so glad she came with me.

When we arrived in Nairobi Lois was at the airport to meet us with a driver. It was about an hour's drive to Lois's darling little cottage, and the driver helped us unload the bags into her house. As we drove into the estate, there were *askaris* (guards) at the gate who let us in. The gardens were colourfully profuse, with bougainvillea, roses and beautiful flower beds, and outside Lois's cottage huge avocado and mango trees, laden with fruit. Lois offered us drinks and we sat down to relax on the verandah which was shaded by a vivid purple bougainvillea and several palm trees. It was truly a heavenly spot.

Lois had arranged for Jane and me to go on a short safari to Lake Naivasha: we were going in search of rhino. Our driver drove us around the lake on the sandy shores: we saw many buck, and then he said,

"There it is!" and pointed to a black dot in the distance. We couldn't believe this black dot was a rhino, but as we drove closer we could see it was—he knew what he was looking for. We drove quite close to it, but had to be careful to be downwind, as they are ferocious if they charge.

Lois took us to the famous Mathega Club for lunch. As we walked into the front entrance hall, there was a huge notice board with messages for people and cubby holes where messages could be left.

I was fascinated to see a name from the past—Stuart Vetch. I was at
school with him and my mother bought my favourite horse, Rainbow,
from him. I wished there was a way I could meet him again, but we
were not staying long.

Having lunch in the club was like living in the past. It seemed
so wonderfully formal and old fashioned, with white table clothes
and starched napkins, and the waiters dressed in *kanzoos* (long white
robes) and red *pez* (little hats). The meal was sumptuous, and we relaxed in the garden after lunch. Lois had arranged to play bridge, and
Jane and I went swimming in the pool; we met many other ex-pats
who were there with their children.

During our last week in Kenya, Lois arranged another safari
to the Aberdare National Park and the Mount Kenya National Park.
We left Nairobi early in the morning in a Landrover and drove many
miles on tarmac, which then changed to a rough road until we arrived
at Murang'a; eventually we arrived at the Aberdare Country Club, a
delightful spot with panoramic views. The bedrooms were *rondavels*
scattered around the property, and in the evening we had drinks on the
verandah and met others who were on safari from different parts of
the world. Jane and I arranged to hire horses and ride up amongst the
wild animals. Early the next morning we went down to the stables and
mounted our horses, accompanied by a *syce*. We were very pleased to
find the horses were thoroughbreds, ex-racehorses—I was jolly glad
we could both ride, as it would have been hard for someone inexperi-
enced. We rode up through a track behind the hotel and came out on a
plateau: there in front of us was a herd of zebra, impala, giraffes and
wildebeest. The syce took us right through the animals. We were only
feet away from these wild animals and they did not seem at all per-
turbed that we were there. We were informed there was no ferocious
game in the park.

The following day we went to Mount Kenya National Park
and stayed in a wonderful hotel on stilts. It was built on the edge of a
waterhole, with a verandah running around the edge so people could
watch the animals coming for water. They had a bleeper system in all

the rooms—if it was an animal worth coming to see it would bleep once; if it was an elephant or lion, it would bleep twice; if it was a leopard it would bleep three times. We sat for hours watching the animals come down to drink as the sun was setting, and the waterhole was lit up at night. When we were ready for bed, we knew we would be called if something exciting came to drink. We were thrilled to be called with three bleeps and rushed down in our dressing gowns to see two buffalo and a leopard: leopards are so rare to see.

On our return to Lois's cottage, we packed up our things for our return to France the next day. I certainly felt much better and stronger. It was a pleasant, unhurried visit; we saw a lot and relaxed and had many tales to tell our friends.

Although I never did find out what caused the pernicious anaemia, it would not surprise me one bit if someone told me it was to do with the stress and overwork of the scout event. I wonder if I have a genetic predisposition for it, as my cousin David also suffers from the condition.

***

I tend to get rather attached to the horses I ride, and Jean-Charles was always looking for ideal horses. He acquired a beautiful bay mare that I became very fond of, and one day she was gone. I asked,

"Where is Erie?" and he replied,

"I sold her to the hunt for Daguet." I could have cried, I was so sad to see her go, but was pleased to see her out at the hunt. Three months later, I arrived at the hunt, ready to do my relay, and someone asked me if I wanted the mare. And I said,

"I would love to have her." I never dreamt of ever owning my own horse, never mind this beautiful mare. As we were returning to the rendezvous, Madame d'Ailliè res rode up next to me and said,

"I hear you want the mare; you can have her at the end of the season."

Well, I could hardly believe my ears: here I was agreeing
to buy a mare, and now I had to find somewhere to keep her. I telephoned Diana and asked if they had any space at the stables where
she kept her horse. Luckily there was, but Erie would be going out to
grass for the summer and returning in August.

Mme d'Aillières agreed a very good price to buy the horse,
and she also arranged a very favourable fee for me to pay to hunt
once a week. I was over the moon, and had three wonderful years of
hunting with Erie. She was a very strong comfortable ride—probably
more suitable for a man, as she was so large and powerful, but I had
so much fun on her. I taught her to canter and gallop instead of the
fast trot, which was the main pace of these trotters. She also learnt to
jump: we didn't have fences out hunting, but it was handy going over
trees and ditches. Most of the French trotters clamber over trees rather
than jump them.

I rode her most days except the day after hunting, when I let
her rest. It was wonderful exercise and we had the most beautiful
rides in the forests. I only ever fell off her three times, and each time
was so unexpected. She was not prone to shying and she was always
eager to go, whether on her own or with other horses. The first occasion she dumped me was when we passed a cottage in the forest
with extremely loud music, and, like a cork coming out of a bottle,
she exploded. The next time, I was riding alone and she was trotting
along with not a care in the world, and I never saw what made her
explode—I landed on my feet next to her, but as soon as I touched the
reins, which were still in my hands, she bolted, and that was a long
walk home. The third time was a week after the St Hubert at the Chateau de Compiegne, where we had a joint meet with five others hunts
to celebrate the last St Hubert of the century. Again, we were trotting quietly and we had just passed a fallen tree when she exploded,
but this time I fell rather heavily and she stopped and started eating
grass. I got myself up, picked up my phone that had fallen out of my
pocket, and walked over to her, calling her name quietly. She looked
up and the reins flapped and that sent her off at full gallop, back to the
stables. I rang the stables and they said she had just arrived back, and

did I want someone to come and collect me. I agreed that it would be a good idea, as I was rather sore and had a long walk.

When I returned to the stables, Florence had unsaddled her and she was standing in her box. I checked her over, rubbed her down and put on her rug for the night. I knew I was in no fit state to hunt the next day, so I offered her to a friend who was recovering from a broken collarbone. She was at the peak of her fitness and needed the exercise. I had asked my friend not to hunt her more than three hours, but as it turned out the hunt only lasted 40 minutes; however, when I went back to the stables to see her, she was totally lame.

I called a vet and scans were taken. I had to keep her in the box for three weeks and then I could take her out for ten minutes every day, to walk her around. She never seemed to recover, she spent the whole winter in her box; she had just been clipped before the St Hubert, so I couldn't put her out in a field to recuperate. Every time I took her out for ten minutes, I had to sedate her so she wouldn't explode outside her box. She was like a spring ready to erupt. The vet suggested she go out into fields for the summer and see how she was at the beginning of the season again.

It was the 30th April and she was going out on 1st May; I dosed her with a sedative to take her out one last time. I may not have given her enough time for the sedative to work. I let her graze some of the grass just near the manège, and then she suddenly exploded violently. Someone shouted,

"*Laisser les reins, laisser les reins.*" I let go of the reins and she stopped; she went back to eating grass, but on three legs. I could have cried. We had nursed her all these months, for her to go and do this. I led her back to her stable on three legs, and Diana was in her box with her horse. I just said,

"Please can you call the vet? She can't go on like this." I couldn't actually say "please put her down," but Diana knew what had to be done. I gave my precious Erie one last hug and a kiss on her nose, called Jicky and went to my car, tears pouring down my face. I couldn't speak to anyone, I was so distraught and upset. I could not go back to the stables for nine months; I had too many memories that I could not deal with yet.

On the second Sunday in June, the Prix de Diane Hermès (the French Oaks) was held in Chantilly. This is a very prestigious Group 1 race meeting, sponsored by Hermès. Anna's lunches, which they became known as, really began back when I was working for Freddie Head, when I invited Diana and Ben and Pat Ryan and their children from Paris and we had a very nice lunch in my garden and then went off to the races. This is an occasion to wear hats and look very glamorous.

The following year I had my new garden and I invited some local friends, a friend from England, and some of my diplomat clients from Paris. We had two tables of eight and I laid on a very nice cold buffet with hot new potatoes with mint and butter, followed by straw-berries and cream, a crème brûlée and a pavlova. We then went off to the races, where I had been able to acquire Main Stand tickets.

The next year it rained and I had to quickly put up a Scout tent for cover; the year after I rented a tent, as I had about thirty people for the lunch. That was when I realized I need to buy a tent, and the tent hire firm offered me the one I had been using for a reduced price. Anna's Prix de Diane lunches were becoming a tradition, and they seemed to get bigger and better every year. I even heard that someone had asked a friend how much it cost to come to one my lunches. The regulars were invited every year and there were always new people to invite. It was a very stressful day for me, as I usually had another two lunches to deliver and sometimes even arrange for a cook to be there to serve it at a trainer's residence.

Every year the Prix de Diane had a different national theme: for the year 2000 it was Scotland, and I was very involved with the company Terre d'Ecosse that represented Scotland in France. I had met Jonathan Findlay in 1998 when he was looking for a caterer for his Scottish events for Terre d'Ecosse. We immediately felt a kindred

Picnic at Prix de Diane, 2000

Racecourse at Chantilly, Prix de Diane, 2000

Jane enjoying the garden

Wedding tea in my front garden

Prix de Diane Lunch

Anna, Prix de Diane lunch

Anna with Harriette and Charlotte

Charlotte, at tea time

spirit, especially when I learned he was at Glenalmond, where my father had attended school, before serving as an Officer in the Scots Dragoon Guards. We worked together on many big events all over France: the *XVIIeme Journées de la Chasse et de la Pêche* (the Game Fair) at Chambourg, the Four Nations Rugby, World Cup Football at the new *Stade de France* in Paris, and various other events on the Seine and in historic buildings in Paris and on the east coast.

This year I decided to do my lunch differently: I would hold a picnic in the Hermès parking area on the racecourse. I brought all the food and tables and cloths, champagne and wine, asked my guests to bring a fold-up chair, and issued them with special parking tickets into the Hermès parking area. This was a spectacular affair, not seen very often in France. The traffic on the roads to the racecourse were always jammed on Prix de Diane day, and we always had to rush to get there in time for the races, but on this day we were right on site. After lunch we wandered over to the main stand to watch all the extra activities as well as the racing. They had the Scots Dragoon Guards playing, a tossing the Cayber event, and an exhibition of Scottish wolf hounds, all arranged by Jonathan and Terre d'Ecosse.

The picnic idea worked so well that I decided to do the same thing the following year. Sadly, that was the last Prix de Diane lunch I was to hold; I have heard that everyone misses Anna's Prix de Diane lunches.

***

One of the major problems of having poultry was Mr. Fox. He came round expecting dinner for his family, and if I was not careful to close up the chickens, ducks and geese he would come round and kill as many as he could. Sometimes I would be lucky and find some bedraggled bird that came out of hiding in the morning. It was so sad, and broke my heart. All my birds had names.

One day I was working in the garden and I heard the geese making a frightful noise: I rushed over to their pen and found a fox trying to haul Charlotte over the fence. I shouted and he dropped his prey and ran. I rushed over to Charlotte who was lying there, as if dead. She was bleeding, and I saw a wound on the back of her neck. I had a problem, as I had just sent my chef off with my van and had no transport; so I picked her up and ran upstairs to call a friend to come and pick me up and take us to the vet's office. My friend came round and I rushed into the vet's, asking if they could help save Charlotte. They admitted they had never had a goose as a patient, but they would do the best they could for her.

She was at the vet's for five days: I went in every day to feed her by hand, as she still couldn't lift up her head. It was a bank holiday weekend coming up and the vet had no other patients, so she asked if I would take her home and nurse her there. I had a large cage that I put her in and Harriette was so pleased to see her, she just sat next to her and kept making grunting sounds. The next morning Charlotte lifted her head briefly and ate by herself. I am sure that being home with Harriette speeded up her recovery: it wasn't long before she was back to normal and able to join the rest of the birds again.

***

During this time I was very sad to hear that Lois had died in Kenya, at the age of 84. It seemed that she had been ill for a short while and was taken into hospital, where she recovered enough to be sent back to her cottage. A few days later she became ill again and I believe she died in the ambulance going to the hospital. I was very thankful that she had not suffered a long lingering illness.

David, Penny and Jamie went over to Kenya to arrange her affairs and cremate her body so they could return with the ashes. Unfortunately, the crematorium had recently burnt down, so they were offered the Hindu pyre. When they arrived at the pyre they had a brainwave that Lois would have approved of—they took her covered body out of the coffin and laid it on the pyre and returned the coffin to get their money back. Some may be horrified by this, but anyone who knew Lois would know that she would be up there saying "Well done, you chaps!" All her life she had been thrifty and couldn't bear waste of any sort.

I was very sad that the day they chose for her memorial service and to have her interred was the day after Christmas. My busiest periods were the days leading up to Christmas and Boxing Day. Of course, Lois had her own three children and many grandchildren: there were many people to be considered and I know I was low down on the pecking order. I felt she had been my mother for the last 32 years, and I suffered deeply from not being able to attend the service.

***

I always felt that I needed a showcase for the cakes and food I was preparing, and I wondered if a British-style tea room would work in Chantilly. I found an ideal shop right on a corner with traffic lights which sold clothes, sort of red-light district clothes, not what you would expect people in Chantilly to wear. I boldly went in and asked the proprietor if she was interested in selling up, but she refused. I still yearned for this shop, and not long afterwards, a friend who knew about my interest telephoned me and said if I still wanted it I should make an offer as soon as possible, as the shop was going into liquidation.

"Hurrah!" I thought, and telephoned a friend of mine who spoke far better French than I did, and we went in to chat with the same person I had spoken to a few weeks before. We then went to see the estate agents and agreed a figure. Helen joined me in partnership, and while we were setting up the company she mentioned the Redesdale in passing and admitted that she had been there the year after me. What a coincidence! We had to apply for a "change of use" permit, as we wanted to be able to cook and serve food: there were very strict rules and regulations we had to adhere to, but eventually The English Shop was opened as a tea room with simple pub-type lunches. We also sold English products: food, magazines, cards, gifts, and a whole range of fresh cakes, scones and quiches. We also made and sold Marks-and-Spencer-type sandwiches that were very popular for people on the run. English Sunday papers were very popular, as were the English brunch on Sundays.

During the first year, Helen and I worked in the shop all day and every day except Mondays; eventually we found it was easier to do the cooking in my prep kitchen and deliver the food every day. I also continued with my outside catering. The English Shop became an institution in Chantilly, a nice place for girls to meet for lunch or even alone—everyone always felt comfortable there. Sunday was a particularly busy day with many tourists coming to see the Chateau and Horse Museum.

Before we had organized our deliveries from England, Helen and her husband, John, drove over to the UK and physically picked up all the fresh goods, groceries, magazines, etc. It was one Sunday very soon after we opened, that they went over for the delivery; I had my cousins Jenny and Miles Lloyd (both ex-Kenyans) staying, and they came and gave me a hand in the shop. It turned out to be our busiest day so far, and I was thankful they were there to help. Miles was in the kitchen churning out English breakfasts, teas and coffees; Jenny was our waitress and I had to do the till. What a day we had! Customers never stopped coming in. It was an August bank holiday weekend and coach loads of tourists stopped at the Chateau and walked down into the town, thankful to find a nice cosy tea room. A party from England asked the price of a picture we had on the wall and with no hesitation I said I would find out, and I disappeared into the backroom to ponder this problem.

Helen had been taking framing classes and had a selection she was putting together for an exhibition, and to brighten up our walls she decided to hang some in the shop. This particular picture was of three famous race horses, taken from the centre of a magazine and then framed beautifully by Helen. I picked up the telephone and started dialing Helen's cell phone, hoping I would catch her before she entered the Chunnel and she lost reception, but I was too late: the voice mail asked me to leave a message. Now what? I finally came up with a silly price, assuming that these people wouldn't dream of paying it; I returned to the table where they were enjoying their brunch and gave them a figure which I was sure they would say was a little too expensive for them.

The English Shop, Chantilly, France

Cakes and English bread

I carried on serving other customers and when these people were ready to leave, I found a pile of French francs on their table and they said "We'll take the picture."

With a big smile I told them I would wrap it up for them. I took it off the wall and went into the back to wrap it up for a coach trip back to UK. I was horrified, and Helen would be furious with me—this was one of her masterpieces for the exhibition. I couldn't believe they accepted the price. I returned with their picture safely wrapped for the trip and thanked them for visiting us.

When Helen and John returned, I had to own up to selling her picture: it wasn't even a painting, just the centre pages of a magazine. At least I had charged enough to give a good profit after the expense of the framework: I warned Helen never to leave anything in the shop she didn't want to sell, as I was sure to sell it!

***

For my next "big" birthday I arranged to hold a party at the club house at the stables where I kept Erie. Several friends helped clean it up and we laid the tables in a U, covered them with white table clothes and laid up the silver. My good friends, Helen Blanc Francard and Clare Belk, made the most beautiful napkin rings of heather and thistles, and we arranged tiny little cyclamen plants and thistles down the centre of the table. My cousins from England, Miles and Jenny Lloyd, brought over helium balloons and covered the ceiling with them. The theme was Scottish: either kilts, black tie or anything tartan was acceptable. Relations and friends came from America, Malta, Scotland, Ireland, England and France.

Jonathan Findlay came with his girl friend Nathalie, and after dinner he showed us all how to do Scottish dancing. He had provided the music and everyone was having such fun trying to learn. At about 1.30 a.m. we heard some real pipes, and three pipers marched into the dance floor. I couldn't believe it: what a surprise! Tears poured down my face, I was so touched. What was so extraordinary was that they actually found us—the club house is buried deep in the forests of Chantilly. It was 11ᵗʰ November, Armistice Day, and these pipers had been playing at the Somme in the morning and Jonathan had hired them to come to play at my party. Perhaps they were due earlier, but as it happened the timing was great. We then tried to teach them to do some Scottish dancing; they were French pipers and really had no idea how to do Scottish dancing.

The evening ended with Geoffrey getting up and reading another of his poems, which was beautifully framed and given to me.

Anna the Bold

This is the story of Anna the Bold,
an inspiring story that should be told.
Ten years ago we did relate,
the epic yarn of Anna the Great.

As years rolled by our Anna became bolder,
until a fall from her horse injured her shoulder.
She suffered so much from the shock and the pain,
that she went right out and did it again!

Yet bolstered still by her supply of cokes,
Anna kept going as well on smokes.
But wait—I hear this is not true,
the fags have gone and the cokes too!
Alas and alack, the little blighter,
she went back to them (to confound the writer!)
Well, it's on with the food and on to the horses,
(with many a tale (ail) between the courses.)

Her menagerie—you have heard of that?
It couldn't be limited to just one cat.

Of cats there are many and a dog on the loose,
and hens and ducks, not to mention the goose.

They live with Anna in the house with the lichen,
it's also the home of Anna's Kitchen.

Let me finish my story as best I can,
I have yet to talk of the little red van.
It trundles around from table to table
Carrying culinary delights, and that's no fable!

So you can believe all that is written,
especially when I say that with Anna we are smitten.

The rest of the tale will have to come later,
for Anna, she's off to cook and to cater.

From all of your admirers, my dearest Mrs Murray,
We love you as strongly as your spiciest curry!

I had a dinner party at the Gate House for the new Head of
Chancery. I stopped off at the English Shop to pick up something for
the dinner, and I found a small boy, sitting outside the door. I asked
him if he wanted to come in, and he said he was waiting for his mother to pick him up. When I saw Helen, she asked if there was a young
boy outside, and I said I had just spoken to him. She had just received
a telephone call from his mother saying she was stuck in traffic in
Paris, so I called the boy in and we gave him a drink and some cake,
and reassured him his mother would arrive as soon as she could.

I continued my journey to Paris, and as I got in the car I
touched the radio switch and it changed channels to the local French
channel. It was announcing that the Firemen were on strike and had
blocked the Périphérique and made fires on the road with barrels

of fuel. The route I was taking would make it necessary to use the Périphérique, to get to the Embassy, so I travelled on a while and took a right turn to reach my normal route, if I left from my house. This way, I travelled along the Seine and then came in to Paris over the Périphérique. I arrived at the Seine at 4 p.m., and I rang Simon at the embassy to say the road was blocked in front of me, and according to the news on the radio, all traffic in Paris was at a standstill. I promised to keep in touch, or he could phone me to check on my progress. An hour later I rang Simon and said I had moved all of ten yards. Very slowly I made progress, and finally arrived at Porte de Clichy where I turned in towards Paris and the dreaded Périphérique. I still had to get across it. In the traffic ahead of me was a Fire Vehicle which had been turned into a bandstand with very loud live music and amplifiers. When I spoke to Simon, he asked,

"Are you really in a traffic jam, or at a party? It sounds like you are having a great time!"

I assured him that it was the fire brigade and their demonstrators. It was now 8 p.m. and his dinner guests would be arriving, and I still had not arrived at the Périphérique—when I did finally reach it, the police were there and directing me away from it. I found a little road and I managed to get over the Périphérique, but on the other side the traffic was still at a standstill. I was about ten minutes from the Embassy, in normal circumstances. Simon rang me to say he was trying to book his party into a restaurant; I told him I still wanted to come to the Embassy, as I was desperate to use the bathroom and there was no way I could stop where I was—the road was too narrow. I would just have to continue and try to get back on course. I eventually arrived at the Embassy at 9.15 p.m. and was greeted by Simon at the door.

"I thought you were going to a restaurant?" I said.

"I couldn't find one that could take a party of 14 at short notice, so I ordered pizza. Now that you are here, we will have our original starter and your salad, cheese and dessert—I realize there is no time to cook the main course and pizza is on its way." It was the strangest meal I ever laid a hand to at the Embassy: pizza served on silver salvers by waiters in white jackets and bow ties. To make it more interesting, one of the guests was Tony Allen-Mills, who writes for the Sunday Times, and the following week there was a very funny story about this dinner. Oddly enough it was one of my friends who showed me the cutting and asked,

"Could this be you?" The story of my trip to Paris had got around. I think I probably gained a few grey hairs and I certainly bit all my nails. This was living on the edge.

***

Three major events in my life happened in 2001. The first was losing my beloved Erie—it took me a long time to get over that. The second was my landlords' decision to sell up, due to ill health, which meant I would have to find somewhere else to carry out my Anna's Kitchen activities. I was very sad to be leaving my little house with the garden I had restored and nurtured, and the wonderful Prep kitchen I had built in what used to be the stables. I was due to hand over the keys on the 14th of July, so I worked hard to make sure the garden was looking lovely and all my belongings were moved out. The week leading up to my departure, it rained and rained and rained—in thirteen years there, I had never seen so much rain. I watched as the river flooded its banks and crept up my lawn. Friends helped me fill sand bags and put them round the kitchen door: it was on ground level, with no step, so had no protection if the water rose any more. The water was already five feet from the kitchen door. We had two days without rain and then I woke to the most enormous thunderstorm and pouring rain again. When I went to feed the geese, chickens and ducks, they ushered me into the potting shed, as the thunder cracked overhead and the lightning lit up the dark morning sky. I was standing in the potting shed filling the feed bowls, which I was going to leave there out of the wet, when there was an almighty crack and roar: I looked out of the potting shed to see four or five very large poplars falling like dominoes. The tips of the trees were just feet away from us, right across my beautiful croquet lawn.

The trees were normally on the edge of the river, but for days had been under water: this final storm had completely loosened them

Diana in front of the house at Gouvieux

The day before the rains

Jicky, Harriette the goose, Phantome the cat and some of
the hens

The river broke its banks, heaven for the geese and ducks

Flooding almost reached the house

Finale - the poplar trees fell like dominoes on my lovely
lawn

and torn them down. This is when I gave up—I knew I could fight no more for my little home. It was time to move on.

***

The Internet was becoming a thing that everyone talked about, and since I really needed a computer for my work, I also got connected to the Internet. I really had no idea why I needed the Internet at that stage, but it was fun exploring it. I remember it well: I switched on, and then had no idea what or where I was going or doing. I put my cousin's name in the search tool and a whole list of addresses came up for her, so I sent her an e-mail, and I was so excited when I got a reply very shortly afterwards. She welcomed me and said that it was a good idea to put something in the subject line, as she might have just deleted it. My first lesson, all the way from Florida!

While exploring, I found Bridge, so I went into the bridge room, and then I found it was possible to watch by kibitzing at tables and how it worked. Well, it wasn't long before I got involved and started playing, and that was the beginning of my addiction to online Bridge. I got very friendly with many players and even met some who came to Paris. This was a really fun way to meet nice people who had the same interest.

One of my favourite Bridge partners was Halvard: his ID was Haro. He and his wife, daughter and son-in-law, came to Paris for a visit; we met up at their hotel and visited several museums and places of interest. We had a picnic in the grounds of Les Invalids, and then we played bridge on the lawn until the gendarmes came and asked us to move on. We had so much fun that Halvard invited me to come to Norway and stay a week in their cottage up in the Fjords.

In the meantime, I had some other lovely friends in Canada and the USA, and they all were all urging me to visit as well. I began thinking about making a trip to North America, but in the meantime I planned a visit to Norway and had the most marvelous time in the mountains at Halvard's cottage. As the plane took off from Charles de Gaulle airport, the Captain announced that due to a strike by the loading crew, some of our luggage may not get through on this trip.

We arrived at Oslo and I found I was one of the unlucky ones with
no luggage. I was instructed to carry on with my trip to Trondheim
and report my missing luggage when I arrived. Halvard and Auslag
greeted me with smiling faces at the airport: I told them about my lost
luggage and we went and reported it. I filled in the necessary forms
with the address for my bags to be sent, and they handed me a packet
with a t-shirt, wash things and tooth brush to tide me over.

The drive out of Trondheim up towards the mountains was full
of breathtaking views; eventually we came off the main roads on to a
dirt track, and finally a small bridge that had no guard rails and was
no wider than the car—the water was only a few inches below and
would be impassable with any flooding. We continued over the bridge
for about half a mile and it really felt like we had come to the end
when Halvard parked the car. I asked where the house was and they
pointed: two kilometers up the hill. Fortunately my hiking boots were
in the small bag I had kept with me on the plane; Auslag and Halvard
had theirs in the boot of the car. We all donned our boots for the first
of several trips back and forth to carry their shopping back to the
house: it was quite a climb.

As we got closer, I could see the cabin had a grass-covered
roof; I had seen many of these on our way here. The cabin was tiny,
with a little covered porch leading onto a deck; the table was an enormous flat rock, surrounded by stools made of wood stumps. It was
charming, and the view was awe-inspiring. Below us there was a lake
and the mountain slopes descended in a steep drop on all sides. Once
we had brought everything up and unpacked the shopping, Halvard
offered us drinks which we enjoyed on the deck. Although it was July,
it was cool enough to wear sweaters. Auslag prepared a wonderful
Norwegian meal with reindeer meat—it was delicious.

I was shown the geography of the place. There was an outside
loo, or longdrop as we used to call them in Kenya. The water was a
tap on the side of the house, fed by the nearby stream running down
the mountain. We filled up pans to heat on the gas stove for washing
up and washing ourselves. Halvard had installed solar panels for light

ing, and as it stays light very late in the summer we didn't need them for long in the evenings.

I borrowed clothes from Halvard and Auslag and we hiked along a mountain ridge one day, enjoying more spectacular views, and then a beautiful rainbow appeared from nowhere. Halvard carried a little wooden dish attached to his belt and when we were thirsty we would find running water and stop for a drink, using this utensil.

We drove to a spot where we could leave the car and then hiked down the mountain until we came to a sparkling waterfall. It was very high but not very wide. The three of us sat down in the long grass and Halvard pulled out the cards and bidding boards and we played three handed bridge right in front of the waterfall. After a good rest and playing a few hands of bridge, Auslag returned up to the car and Halvard and I continued. We crossed three enormous rivers using a rope bridge, which swung in the wind as you were crossing. It was quite terrifying. Once we had negotiated the three rivers there was a steep mountain ahead of us. Halvard led the way and pulled himself up on a rope that was hanging down the mountain. He told me to do the same: when I got to the top, he grabbed my hand and pulled me onto the ledge. After a bit more climbing we came out into a field full of wild flowers, and some barn-like buildings in the distance. I was so exhausted I lay down in the sweet-smelling grass surrounded by the flowers, and then I heard Auslag's voice—she had driven around the mountains to collect us on the other side.

On my third day, we drove into town where Halvard's parents lived, on the other side of our mountain on the edge of a Fjord. My luggage was being delivered there as they lived in a regular street, and it also gave us a chance to have a longed-for shower. We spent the night there and played bridge with his parents, taking it in turns one at a time to sit out.

Another day Halvard drove us to the opening of a valley and parked the car. We hiked for hours between the mountains up the valley, over streams and stopped to chat to some sheep grazing by the riverside.

The skies were azure blue, and as the morning warmed up we took off our sweatshirts and tied them around our waists. Eventually we came to a small wooden house with a large table in the front yard: the table was made from a tree trunk, with smaller sections of tree trunks making bench seats. We flopped down on the seats, tired and thirsty. A young girl came out of the house and asked us if we would like refreshments. She brought us fresh milk and yogurt and crusty bread. It was delicious and most refreshing. We paid the family for their hospitality and went on our way, back down the valley.

I enjoyed every moment of my visit, discovering such a charming unspoiled country where old habits won't die. After my return from Norway, I began to make plans for visiting North America. Two of my really good bridge friends were Paul in the U.S. and Kim in Canada, so I arranged to come over to the U.S. and meet up with Paul, and then together we would drive to Canada to meet Kim and her husband Mike, who also played bridge.

I remember when Paul met me at Dulles airport: he had a bunch of flowers in his hand and a big smile on his face. He helped me with my cases and we stepped out into the lovely warm air. He took me for a meal in Leesburg while we chatted and got to know each other. We left early the next morning for Canada: during the week we visited Kim and Mike, we really became close. A trip to Niagara Falls was arranged and we had a very nice meal in a revolving tower overlooking the falls. Kim and Mike took us to dinner at their local Club, which was charming—it was a little old fashioned, but served delicious food. Both Paul I had a great week with Kim and Mike, and we have stayed friends ever since.

On our return to Virginia, we visited Paul's parents and I met his sister and brother-in-law, Diane and Jeurgen, who were visiting from Germany. The family was charming and very welcoming. When it was time for me to leave and return to France, Paul persuaded me to come back. I had to return. I had met his family, his parents and his sister Diane and her husband, and everyone was so nice, it was an easy decision to make.

I eventually moved over here to be with Paul on the 11th of September, 2001. I had sent my dog Jicky and Guinness the cat the day before, as their flight left later than mine: I wanted to put them on the plane, as I knew they would be very frightened. They arrived that afternoon and Paul collected them from the Airport at Dulles. I was to arrive the following afternoon.

CHAPTER 6

AMERICA

I held a sale in my tent of all my Anna's Kitchen equipment and electrical items that would not be compatible in the United States, and moved in with my friend Diana. I was sending a shipment of my belongings by sea, and the shippers were collecting everything from Diana's house on Monday afternoon. I sold my beloved little red Anna's Kitchen van that had become part of the establishment, and I was very sad to see it go to its new owners. All that was left was for me to pack my bags. Diana took me to the airport very early on Tuesday morning, 11th September 2001.

I arrived at Heathrow around 9 a.m. and met my brother for breakfast; I had about three hours to kill before my flight took off for Dulles, Virginia. Andrew waved me goodbye as I went to board my flight. Shortly after takeoff, we were offered drinks and pretzels and then our meal was brought round, and most people settled down to watch a film or show on the individual monitors.

I decided to get some sleep after I had watched a film, as we still had a few hours to go before landing at Dulles. It had been a long day, as we had to leave Diana's house at 5 a.m. for check-in at Charles de Gaulle airport. I was dozing when the loudspeaker announced that due to a technical hitch, we would be landing in Gander in Newfoundland, Canada. The Captain also announced to check where our nearest Exit was. I looked out of the window and saw marshland below us, and now I was waking up and thinking, 'Oh my gosh, there must be something wrong with the plane, that we are being diverted and reminded to check where the Exits were! Not only that, why are we flying to Uganda—I thought we were flying to Dulles, USA?' I had never heard of Gander, Newfoundland.

Passengers were beginning to talk and we wondered what was going on. When we landed the plane seemed to be working its way around other planes before it came to a standstill. Once we had stopped, the Captain announced,

"If you are looking out of the window and seeing planes landing every minute, you must be wondering if they all have technical hitches. Two different planes have crashed into the Twin Towers, and the American airspace has been closed down." Utter confusion broke out on the plane, and we were asked to try and keep calm, and we would be informed of any updates as soon as the Captain heard anything. A short while later he announced that a plane had crashed into the Pentagon; some time later he told us about the plane that went missing in Pennsylvania.

We were offered our "tea snack" and reminded that stocks were limited, but water would be handed around every hour and we were to keep our plastic cups. The doors of the plane were opened up to give use air, but we couldn't leave the plane, it was twenty feet down to the ground. After several hours the police came round to the plane and threw up some crayons and games for the children, but we still couldn't leave the plane. We were on the plane for 15 hours before the tannoy announced,

"Ladies and gentlemen, we will be disembarking shortly. Please take your hand luggage, pillow and blanket, and have your passports ready." It was 4 a.m. in the morning. Steps were brought round to the plane for us to disembark and school buses were waiting to take us to the airport building, which was more like a shed than an airport terminal. Our passports were checked and then we found a long table with brown paper packets on them, containing sandwiches and drinks and fruit. We each took one, but even though it had been many hours since we had food I found it quite difficult to eat at that hour.

We all boarded school buses again and we were driven into the town of Gander, which was a one-horse town. We arrived at a school and were shown in, and told to find somewhere to sleep on the floor. In the Gymnasium/hall, they had set up an enormous television, and another one in the library. I don't think anyone could sleep: we needed to let people back home know that we were ok, and where we were. Telephones had been installed on the sidewalks, on the ground, for people to use.

When I rang my brother, no one was home; everyone was at work. I rang Paul at around 5 a.m. and woke him: he was so relieved to hear my voice, and I reassured him I was okay. I then went into the main hall and watched the television. It was mesmerizing, and so utterly devastating. We were crying watching it. I knew I probably knew no one in the buildings, but the loss of life was just horrific. I just prayed that my fellow companions were not watching loved ones hurtling to their deaths. It was truly the most horrific, tragic disaster I've ever seen, and I hope never to encounter anything like it again.

When we started seeing repeats again, I decided I must try and get some sleep. I had been awake for about 30 hours. The hard classroom floor was very uncomfortable, with just the small pillow from the aircraft and the thin blanket. I considered myself lucky, though, as I had met an elderly gentleman, who had recently had a hip replacement and the floor would be extremely uncomfortable for him. The following day, I found they had wonderful communications in the school, computers everywhere, so I was able to get online and communicate with many friends, who were wondering where I had got to.

The Canadians are the most wonderful people: they kept a supply of hot food running all day. Ladies came in with various delicious steaming dishes, and food was available at any hour of the day or night. The local store donated piles of new underwear for everyone, and residents brought in razors, soap, toothbrushes, toothpaste, jeans, sweaters, t-shirts and all sorts of necessary toiletries. Their generosity was amazing, and no one had to do without. I was having trouble with swollen legs: I had packed my elasticated stockings in my main luggage, and my legs were beginning to suffer. When I mentioned this to the Red Cross nurse, she brought me a new pair of stockings a few hours later, and refused to let me pay for them. On the second night in Gander, the locals brought in blankets; it wasn't very cold, but at least we could use them to sleep on. On the third night, the army came in with cots and we each received one to sleep on. This made it far more comfortable.

2001 - Paul and me celebrating my birthday   Anna at Warrenton Under the Stars

My favourite restaurant

Everyone congregated into the two rooms with the televisions that Friday for the memorial service. There wasn't a dry face to be seen. It was heart-wrenching and just so terribly sad that so many could die in this terrorist attack. No one will ever forget 9/11.

The following morning, Saturday, we woke to hear the loudspeaker announcing that the airspace had been opened up, and our plane would be leaving at 7 a.m. We packed up our meager belongings and waited outside the school for the buses to arrive.

We had rather a long wait once we boarded the aircraft—there really did seem to be a technical hitch and mechanics had to be called. Eventually we took off with a cheer and clapping from all the passengers. Everyone was so relieved to be on the way again. As we approached Dulles, the Captain warned us that we would be the first aircraft coming in since the airspace was opened, and there would be an enormous amount of press waiting to talk to people.

I kept my head down, and saw Paul, tall and handsome, standing at the back. I made straight for him, so relieved to have arrived at last. We arrived home to see my precious dog and cat, well settled in and perfectly happy in their new surroundings, and Paul's cat, Lucky, not at all fazed by either Jicky or Guinness.

It wasn't long before I realized how much I missed working and earning my own living. It was not easy getting a job without a work visa, and I had to keep returning to the U.K. to renew my three-month visas. Paul asked me to marry him three times, but I wasn't sure I felt committed enough, to say yes.

In the local paper I found a job as a line cook at a pub/restaurant: I had never heard of a line-cook and hoped it was something I could do. An appointment was made for an interview, and the Executive Chef telephoned me in the evening and thanked me for attending. After consideration, he had found a suitable team member, but asked if I minded if he kept my name on record.

The British Embassy in Washington offered me a job cooking at the Ambassador's residence. I spent three weeks on a trial period. A very pleasant three-bedroom apartment in the residence was offered to me, and I was allowed to bring Jicky. I did not enjoy living in the city, although there was a wooded area opposite to walk the dog. When I didn't stay over, the commute was excruciatingly long and tedious. One of the pluses was the Embassy would be able to get me a work permit.

In the meantime I received another phone call from the restaurant, asking me to go for another interview; I was asked to start work the following Monday. On Mother's Day I had baked a delicious cake for Paul's mother and we were going around for a meal in the afternoon. I received another phone call from the restaurant, asking if I could start that day, so I sent Paul off with the cake and my apologies, and I started my first day at the pub.

My days at the pub began as a chef in the kitchen, and with it a whole knew language. Terms I had never heard of cropped up, and some of the English words I used left people mystified. I never realized what a high staff turnover there was in the restaurant industry, having never worked in restaurants before, but I believe this is very normal.

I felt very happy to have a nice job that kept me occupied. My relationship with Paul was rocky: things came to a crux when he took me to the airport for my flight back to attend Jonathan and Nathalie's wedding in Scotland. He was supposed to be coming with me, but said his mother was so sick, he didn't feel he could leave her. She was very ill, bravely enduring chemotherapy and the loss of all her hair. Before I left, I made sure there was food prepared in the freezer for Paul to take out daily and food for the animals. All the laundry was done. He drove me to the airport and announced,

"I will be entertaining someone else while you are away." I was so shattered, I didn't know what to say. I had to go on, as the flight would not wait: I said nothing at all, and we drove the rest of the way in silence. Terrible thoughts were going through my brain: he had my animals and all my belongings were there. I sat in the car with these screaming thoughts going through me, but I knew there was nothing I could do at this moment. When we arrived at the airport, I collected my bags and left without a word. I checked in and went through all the security systems and then had a long wait for my plane. I had to talk to someone: I rang Diane, Paul's sister, who was staying with his parents. I told her what he had told me, and she said she was so sorry.

The trip to London seemed extraordinarily long, mainly because I had so much to digest. I had to make excuses for Paul all the way—my brother had arranged a huge family party in his garden to meet Paul, and he was expected at the fabulous wedding in Scotland. I decided the best way to deal with it was to be honest and just say Paul had dumped me.

A week before my return, I rang Mimi, who was Sandy Lerner's (my boss) best friend and colleague at the pub and told her the situation. She asked me to ring back the following evening. She told me to get a taxi to the pub and everything would be taken care of when I got there. I was so relieved, as I didn't have the finances to pay for hotels and cars etc., and I had to get back to my precious dog and cat. It was breaking my heart that I had left them there with Paul. He was an animal lover, so hoped he would look after them.

As soon as I arrived at the pub, Sandy was there to meet me, and told me to get the taxi to follow her Range Rover back to the farm, where I was shown to a spare room, and as I was unpacking my things, there was a knock at the door. A man stood there and handed me some keys and said they were for the black jeep, outside, for me to use. I was very grateful, as now I could go and collect my animals.

I drove over to Paul's house and found it locked up (for the first time ever) but I found Guinness outside, so I scooped him up and took him with me. When I got back to the farm I telephoned Paul and said I wanted to come and collect Jicky and I would arrange another time to come and collect all my belongings. I returned and collected Jicky, and came back two days later for everything else. I rented a storage facility, and two men from the farm came to help me move everything. It all went smoothly and amicably, and I couldn't wait to get out of there.

The strange thing is I still had a soft spot for Paul, although nothing on this earth would make me change my mind now. I was sad to lose the friendship of his parents and his sister and brother-in-law, although in fact Diane and Jeurgen have remained friends and I see them on occasions when they visit the U.S.

I concentrated on my job at the pub, which was at times was extremely stressful due to staff shortages, but I didn't really mind. This was my life now and I was going to make the best of it. I stayed in the main house on the farm for six months, and then I moved to a house in Winchester. It was a long drive to work, but much cheaper living than in the neighbourhood of the pub.

Neighbours of Paul's parents, who were renting Diane and Jeurgen's house, found a stray cat in their garden and asked me if I would take it, as they really didn't want to have a cat. They said it was very nervous and seemed to be fairly blind. It was a beautiful white cat, and apparently very friendly, so we arranged for them to come over on my day off so that I could give it undivided attention. It was a Monday just before Christmas, and while they were still there, I had a telephone call from work asking if I could go in to work, as we were short staffed; so I had to abandon the idea of being there and hope everyone would get on okay while I was away. I left for work.

Around 8 p.m., there was a telephone call for me from Ardith, who had been at my house in the afternoon with the cat, and she said,

"There was a terrible accident this afternoon on route 7, and Paul was killed when his car hit a tree." I was dumb with shock. They said he had a stroke at the wheel. I thought what a sad loss, he was only 53; I was very saddened by the loss, even though we had split up. It was a strange feeling and I completely broke down when I saw him at the viewing. He was so good-looking: I could not believe such a large man was lying here in front of me, dead.

Paul's death did not affect me as it might have done. Nothing ever would again. I realized I had been through the worst thing that can happen to a human being: losing a child. Anything after that was possible to bear.

After the funeral, Paul's family asked if I would like to have his cat Lucky, and as both my animals were familiar with him, I agreed. I also agreed to return the white cat, who spent the whole time in the basement hiding and would never come out. He never adapted to our household.

Meanwhile, the restaurant got busier and busier until it was impossible to prepare all the food in the small kitchen in the time before lunch was served. A new prep kitchen was built on the farm; during the transition we used the kitchen in the main house. I injured my shoulder trying to lift a 50lb box of apples off a top shelf and it made it impossible for me to stir soup or sauces, or to lift heavy trays out of the oven.

I saw many doctors, attended physiotherapy, and eventually I was sent to Pain Management where I was given a pain-block injection in my neck hoping it would relieve the pain in my shoulder. The third time I went, where I had to turn up with a driver to take me home, I was told they had not received the okay from the insurers, so after a long wait, I was sent home. The next time I didn't bother getting a driver: I was running out of people to ask, and I felt sure I could manage to drive anyway. It didn't seem so bad, the last time I had one.

As I was given the injection, I suddenly felt very nauseous, and was taken to a bed in a cubicle with curtains around it. I felt myself shivering and becoming feverish; after an hour I only felt worse. They said I had probably developed flu and I ought to go home. I told them my driver was downstairs waiting for me, so I left and gingerly drove myself home. Of course, the one day I really needed a driver, I didn't have one.

I climbed into bed with my electric blanket and shivered. My friend Dean Hess from work rang me to find out how the pain block injection went, and I told him I had a high fever and didn't know what was wrong with me. I rang the Pain Management centre and asked what could have gone wrong: they said it all went well, and I must have flu. Dean came round to my house bearing aspirin. He spent the evening mopping my brow, dosing me up and checking my temperature, making sure I was drinking lots of water. He left me at around midnight when my temperature was almost normal; but that didn't last and I woke up in a sweat again the following day. At around noon Dean rang me again to find out how I was, and I told him I was still running a high fever. He said he was on his way and would take me to the hospital. After checking into the emergency room we waited for what seemed like hours until I was called through and shown to cubicle where my vital statistics were taken and I was seen by a doctor. They could find nothing wrong, but admitted me anyway as my fever was so high.

Dean went back to my house and collected Jicky, my dog, and asked neighbours to feed my cats. I spent four days in hospital and they could find nothing wrong with me, so I was sent home on Sunday and told to contact my family doctor. My house was in a mess: I had had lodgers staying and they had mainly moved out, except they had left large black plastic garbage bags in nearly every room. Half the furniture was theirs, so the house looked empty and dirty without it. I had no energy to go and clean up, so I rang them and asked them to clean out all their things.

On Monday morning I rang my doctor and made an appointment for Tuesday. My doctor gave me a thorough examination and thought I was tender in the abdomen and wanted me to have a cat-scan, which she arranged for the next day. I arrived at the radiology unit and waited and waited. Eventually I asked when I would be seen and was told they were waiting for the okay from the insurers. I said I was feeling so unwell that I would come back another day when they had the okay. I had had to drink some horrible stuff which was disguised as "berry flavoured" before the procedure and I wasn't looking forward to going through this again: I was just going out of the door when they rushed up to me saying they had received the fax with the ok. I was so tired of waiting and was relieved to be ushered into the radiology room.

As I unlocked my front door the telephone was ringing and when I picked it up my doctor said,

"Anna, you need to get back to the hospital. It looks like you have swallowed a fish bone that has perforated your intestine. Go to the hospital and at the front desk tell them you have room 436 reserved for you."

I packed a small bag with necessities and took my laptop. I looked outside to see if there was anyone I could ask to drive me to the hospital, and found no neighbours home, only my car parked outside. I drove to the front entrance of the hospital and left my car there and went into to reception and handed them my car keys and said it was parked outside and could someone please park it and return the keys to me, room 436 was reserved for me. A nurse came round with a wheelchair: I was almost ready to collapse. She took me up to my floor and I was horrified to find it was the cancer ward. Frightening thoughts were flying through my brain—did I have cancer? Was there something she hadn't told me?' However, I was reassured when they told me I was only in this ward because there was no room in the surgical ward. I found the nurses were wonderful here and it was so peaceful. I had surgery on Thursday morning and when I came round I was told Dave Stephens, my general manager from work, was there to see me. I didn't want to see anyone, but I was so touched that he had come to check up on me. When I saw the surgeon I asked about the fish bone, and he said it was a piece of wood.

"Was it a piece of wooden spoon or a chopping board?" I asked. I couldn't imagine how I would swallow a piece of wood.

"No, it was like a little branch, four centimetres long," he indicated, holding up his hand with fingers splayed.

"Could it have been a thyme stem?" I asked. "I was working with thyme and mushroom tartlets in the prep kitchen recently, and perhaps I ingested it."

"Yes, that is exactly what it looked like."

I had the surgery on 10th November and the following Sunday was my birthday: it was a little sad as I didn't imagine anyone knew, and cards from family and friends abroad would be at home. I was so pleasantly surprised when Diane's (Paul's sister) head appeared around the door bearing a lovely bunch of flowers.

"Oh! How nice to see you. How on earth did you know I was here?"

"I brought these flowers around to your house for your birthday and your neighbours told me you were in hospital. We arrived from Germany last week and remembered the 13th."

Diane came with me for my walk around the wards, with my i.v. and walker, and commented, "do you not have a dressing-gown to wear?"

"Well, no, I never have occasion to wear a dressing-gown."

The following day Diane brought me a lovely soft red dressing-gown for me to wear on my walks around the ward.

On Thanksgiving, Dave kindly brought me a delicious dinner from the restaurant, knowing that hospital food would not be very appetising. The surgeon had also been on his rounds and announced that I would probably be able to go home the next day. Unfortunately when the nurses were cleaning my wound, they found it had become infected and sent a swab for analysis; the result showed I had MRSA, which I learnt could be a deadly hospital staph infection. At the time, I had no idea how serious it was or how ill I was. In my room the surgeon numbed my stomach and then cut the scar open so it could drain. I was now being given heavy doses of antibiotics by i.v.; on Sunday when Diane came to visit me, she was very worried and spoke to the nurses. Within minutes I was checked over and rushed into the ICU where everything was so sterile and anyone coming near me, including nurses, had to wear yellow masks, jackets, and gloves. I now had pneumonia and the lung doctor visited me and I was made to inhale a spray, and blow on a little gadget, several times a day, including in the middle of the night—I was woken up frequently to perform these tasks.

I felt the lung doctor was a big bully, although he was only doing his job to help me. To me, he looked like this huge man bullying me into breathing deeper into the blower, and working harder at it.

After a couple of days in ICU, I was returned to a ward, not my lovely cancer ward but instead to the surgical wards. I did miss the peace in the cancer wards; it seemed the nurses held their meetings outside my door at 5 a.m. each day, speaking as loudly as they could. I didn't seem to get any sleep at all being woken with bright lights to blow and inhale, and never at the same time, and then the rude awakening at 5 a.m.

Eventually I was allowed home on the 9th December with my stomach a gaping hole and instructions for nurses to call round twice a day to dress the wound. Three months later I was declared fit enough to resume light duties again and a less heavy-duty job was provided, as hostess in the restaurant. I loved my new job and began to get to know the people I heard about from behind the scenes in the kitchen, but never seen.

I was standing in my usual place receiving guests as they came into the restaurant when I saw a familiar face, but I couldn't put a name to him. He approached with a big smile on his face and said, "How nice to see you looking so well! I am Dr Lewis, and I think you used to call me the 'bully'!" I was astounded, as he looked so big from my bed and yet he was shorter than me in real life.

It was a year after that that the third disaster of my Friday 13th jinx happened. We had a wedding party in the tent on the patio and the rest of the wedding party in the smaller dining room, leaving just the bar, red room and upstairs for the regular Saturday night diners. The evening was extremely busy, with guests queuing up at the bar for tables. I went through to the red room to see if the table for six had been laid for my party sitting at the bar, and I caught my leg on the high chair beside the door. I fell to the ground in agony, and there seemed to be an awful lot of blood. My leg, shoulder and knee hurt, but I wasn't sure of the damage. In the corner of the restaurant, paramedics from the next county were sitting having dinner: they jumped up and came to my rescue, tying my leg up with a table napkin and waiting with me until the ambulance arrived. As I was being lifted up in the gurney, to leave the restaurant, I looked down at a pool of blood: it looked like a murder had been committed.

The journey in the ambulance was very painful and I felt every little bump in the road: I also found out why ambulances have flashing lights and sirens. Every little change of pace is extremely painful, and especially at traffic lights, they try not to stop and start so as to avoid jolting the patient at all. When we eventually arrived at the hospital, my shoulder and knee were x-rayed to make sure no damage was sustained, and they cleaned up my leg. The doctor was holding up something grey and spraying underneath it—when I asked him what it was, he said:

"It is your skin. It is about six by four inches across." It was really a horrible sight. He then proceeded to sew it together, numbing each part of my leg as he went along. I counted 55 stitches. Eventually, cleaned and patched up, I was sent home.

The leg did not heal very well. A large part of my lower right leg died and left a hole with no skin covering it. The first skin graft didn't take, so I had another, a week after my shoulder was operated on. The second skin graft was successful; the shoulder surgery was not.

As a hostess at the restaurant, I try and accommodate everyone I can. Someone might come in and ask for a table for 11, and I would ask them to give me a moment while I arranged it. Looking round for help I would find everyone busy clearing tables, serving food or drinks, so then I would move the heavy teak tables and chairs to make one large table for my guests.

One day in July I felt something pop in my stomach, as I was moving a table. After a moment I realised I probably had a hernia— the wall of my stomach was very weak from my thyme surgery, after the scar had been cut open and left to heal. I returned to the surgeon again and he arranged to repair the hernia the next week.

After having my clips removed, I asked when I could go back to work and he said whenever I liked. So I went back the following day and worked a few hours each day, but after two weeks I felt like the mesh in my stomach had been ripped apart, so the surgeon put me off work for another two weeks.

Every time something horrible has happened to me, my oldest friends tell me it is the Friday the 13th curse striking again. Now I am very careful: I feel like not much more can knock me down, but who knows? I do know that I will not be held down by a curse, if such a curse can be real, or anything else life has to throw at me. I always seem to be able to pick myself up and get on with life. I have a job I really enjoy and I feel very content with my life. There are several people here who have made everything possible for me and helped me through the really hard times: particularly my boss, Sandy, Dave Stephens, Mimi, and Dean. Dean nursed me when I was really sick and took care of my dog for months; he also came to stay every time I came out of hospital and needed someone to stay over. Mimi was the instigator of getting my work visa; Dave has made sure I never wanted for food and was able to pay my bills, and Sandy has given me the most wonderful job, one that I really enjoy. I feel like every day I work at the restaurant is my own private party: I feel the guests are my guests, and so often people have said they feel like they are personal friends of mine. It is a very warm feeling. Life has not been easy here in the U.S., and I am not sure I could have endured it without their help and support. I have stopped bitterly longing the family that was taken away from me, but get pleasure out of seeing other peoples families succeed and enjoying this life. Bridge, both online and in real life, has kept me sane—I am still totally addicted to virtual games, which I can play at any time of night or day. I have visited many parts of the U.S. going to meet online bridge partners and visiting bridge reunions; I was even able to participate in a National American Bridge Championship (NABC).

Wherever I have lived, I have adapted and changed my life to fit in my circumstances, whatever they might offer. I have made many bad decisions in my life, but I don't regret any of them: I have learned from each one. I have been privileged to live in many different places and speak several languages, enjoying traditions, cultures and opportunities too few people ever have the chance to experience. It has been a rollercoaster of a learning curve...but maybe I will always be a little afraid of Friday 13th.